L'Amour Déraisonné
RECLAIMING SELF
Transformational Teachings from Psychosynthesis
and *A Course in Miracles*

Olivia De Gage

Psychosynthesis Press, Mt. Shasta, CA.

L'Amour Déraisonné: Reclaiming Self

Transformational Teachings from Psychosynthesis and *A Course in Miracles*

Copyright 2010 by Olivia de Gage
Cover photo: Abigail DeSoto
Layout: Anahide Mazmanian
All rights reserved

No part of this book may be reproduced in any manner whatsoever without written permission from the publisher, except in the case of brief passages quoted in critical articles and reviews.

ISBN 978-0-9611444-7-0
Library of Congress Control Number: 2010920273

Psychosynthesis Press publishes books that further the full flowering of the human potential in harmony with the interdependent web of life. Psychosynthesis is a transpersonal psychology based on the work of Roberto Assagioli, M.D. (1888-1974) that seeks to integrate all the dimensions of life: physical, emotional, mental, interpersonal, social, ecological, and spiritual. Our books are based in this inclusive, holistic perspective. For information and to order books, visit our web site: PsychosynthesisPress.com.

Psychosynthesis Press
P.O. Box 1301, Mt Shasta CA 96067 • 530-926-0986

No Matter What

I exist no matter what,
No matter what you say or do,
or even what you think…

No matter what you say or do,
or even what you think,
I am the apple of God's eye,
And I am golden.

(Written after a lonely Valentine's Day)

« Le cœur a ses raisons que la raison même ignore. » *Pascal*
(The heart has reasons that even reason knows not.)

TABLE OF CONTENTS

Acknowledgements
Note to the Reader
Preface: Setting the Stage
Introduction: The Path of Love

PART I

Chapter 1   **Crash Landing** .... p. 11
                    The wound

Chapter 2   **Psychosynthesis** .... p. 17
                    Exploring psychosynthesis
                    Subpersonalities
                    My survival personalities

Chapter 3   **The Guardian** .... p. 33
                    Patterns and Conditioning

Chapter 4   **Heartache** .... p. 37

Chapter 5   **Losing Power** .... p. 43

Chapter 6   **Love and All That Jazz** .... p. 47
                    The myth of "falling in love"
                    What we live, by or self interest

PART II

Chapter 7   **Healing** .... p. 59
                    Healing through Tango
                    Loving Kindness

Chapter 8   **A Perfect Day** .... p. 63

Chapter 9   **Day to Day Healing** .... p. 67

Chapter 10 **A New Beginning** .... p. 71
                    Trust and Flow
                    Care and Safety

Chapter 11 **Lost in Incarnation…** .... p. 85
                    Here we go again

Chapter 12 **Holiday Teachings** .... p. 91
                    Christmas Eve
                    Christmas Day
                    The Day after Christmas

Chapter 13 **An Unplanned Change of Plans** .... p. 97
                    Car crash
                    The learning thereof

Chapter 14 **The Decision** .... p. 103

Chapter 15 **Responsibility** .... p. 107
                    (Parental Guidance suggested)

Chapter 16 **"My present happiness is all I see"** .... p. 115

Chapter 17 **Taking time… when it's time** .... p. 119

Afterword
Bibliography & Resources

Acknowledgements

I want to offer a big thank you to Colette Fregeac, my French therapist, and to my American psychosynthesis guide and mentor, Molly Young Brown, without whose consistent help and support I would not have made it through my *"dark night of the soul."*

Special thanks to the French government and people for supporting a socialized health system that allowed me to benefit from the services of a trained therapist and psychologist at minimal cost when I was unable to work for a period of two years. Without this invaluable help I would never have been able to see the family craziness that led to my feelings of inadequacy and unworthiness, and subsequently to release the personal guilt, and "branding" I describe.

A special thank you to John Firman and Ann Gila for their contribution to psychosynthesis through their book, *Psychosynthesis: A Psychology of the Spirit*. Though I never had the opportunity to meet John before his recent death, his work was a godsend to me and I am forever grateful.

Special thanks to Caroline Myss for her dedicated scholarly work in the specialized area of personal development and symbolic sight. I enjoyed meeting her briefly and attending a workshop at the Findhorn Foundation in Scotland in October 2007; her books have been an enormous help to me, as has her unselfish support through CMED's free video workshops and lectures.

Special thanks also to Ken and Gloria Wapnick from A Foundation for A Course in Miracles. Without their amazingly clear and helpful taped lectures and workshops, as well as in person teachings, I am not sure alone I would have grasped the Course's teachings.

And last but not least, a big grateful thank you to Roberto Assagioli, founder of psychosynthesis, or "Papa Assagioli" as I fondly call him, and the continued work, research and practice of psychosynthesis on the part of the dedicated staff at The Psychosynthesis and Education Trust in London (P.E.T.)

Clarification of Terms

psychosynthesis: based on the work of Italian psychiatrist Roberto Assagioli (1888-1974)
"psycho-synthesis" means the synthesis of the psyche.

"Psychosynthesis seeks to understand human psychology by exploring the various components of the psyche... then to bring these components together in a unified, integrated whole so each person can respond creatively and joyfully to the psychological and spiritual demands of life."
          Molly Y. Brown, *Growing Whole*, Introduction

déraisonné: (French) - meaning *"without reason", "unreasonable"* with a trace of insanity.

Note to the Reader

This book is for individuals interested in an interior adventure, those who Jean Houston suggests want to become "archaeologists of the mind." Instead of turning without to the outside world for answers, understanding and wisdom, this book aims at encouraging us to look within.

Sigmund Freud and Carl Jung are among the celebrated pioneers in the field of psychology, offering us roadmaps to the symbolic and unknown world of the human psyche. Roberto Assagioli, Italian psychiatrist, contemporary and student of Freud's, built upon their findings by offering us the practice of psychosynthesis. The story goes that he is said to have responded with delight to Freud's offer to introduce psychoanalysis to the medical community in Italy, with the caveat that he would make some adjustments to the theory. Assiagioli's reply was something like the following:

> *You see, you teach that we are a house with a basement and a first floor; while, in my theoretical house, there is a basement, a first floor, a second floor, a third floor, a sunroof, and an elevator. (1)*

Psychosynthesis provides us not only with a roadmap for understanding our past conditioning and the personality of the self, but offers us an elevator and doorway to take us to the realm of potential, possibility and Self.

We live in a time when the long accepted cultural model of the patriarchy is out-dated, no longer adapted to the challenges that face individuals, societies and most importantly our planet. All of us, regardless of gender, must become aware of the ravages of this imbalance. We have used, abused and trampled the feminine aspects of our being in the same way we have stifled and stepped upon the creative, intrinsic qualities of women and our planet. In response, women are in search of a new understanding of their very beings, far from the rigid containment of the authoritative patriarchal,

NOTE TO THE READER

and the defined roles of "caretaker", "mother", and "nurturer".

The search for the "divine feminine", though far from prevalent, is pushing up like grass through concrete blocks in an urban jungle. Despite the lack of fresh air, sunlight and fertile soil, the unstoppable force of life thrusts its head up to exist. The trampled patriarchically-formatted feminine is doing the same-she can no longer be servant or object; she must stand on her own. At the same time, this "yin" energy has understood that opposing or pushing against the established model is like a dog chasing its own tail. Nothing can be changed through opposition. "Love does not oppose" instructs *A Course in Miracles;* opposition and the use of force only keep us in the framework of traditional "masculine" practices. (2)

The dawning of a new way of being, drawing from both masculine and feminine qualities and values, is emerging, and it is not surprising that women are at its forefront. For centuries women were characterized as "the weaker sex", fragile and in need of stronger male protection. We as women have bowed and honored this model, but today I am struck by the desire, push and motivation of many to discover, create and embrace a new way. Courage, perseverance, attention, patience and creativity are the necessary qualities.

This book is not for people who give lip service to change and personal development. It is one thing to talk about life's journey, change and evolution; it is another to live there. Facing how you live your life with open, honest eyes… exploring egotistical, self-serving motivations, and releasing unloving or unkind attitudes and behaviors opens the door to Assagioli's sundeck; from this vantage point, we have better vision and ability to see what we want to create for ourselves, our families, companies and planet. Recurrent exploration and compassionate understanding allow us to see through the smoke and mirrors of appearance to a hidden world of potential and possibility not yet imagined, but achievable. Our future is up to us.

✶ ✶ ✶

Though not a traditional autobiography, this is a true story. Generally speaking, there are two parts to the book. These parts are not linear or chronological, so the reader may experience a back and

NOTE TO THE READER

forth effect... the feeling of being trapped in past conditioning and pain, then freedom through healing, then rebound into feeling stuck again... This reflects what legitimately happens in emotional healing and change.

Part I explores past pain and its repression in the name of survival. Much of this first section resulted from psychosynthesis exercises and therapy sessions. This exploration allowed me to explore events and feelings that had never been spoken of or recognized. Some of what I recount is symbolic dialoguing using meditation or relaxation techniques. References to childhood trauma have been made in a matter-of-fact, unemotional manner to avoid the feeling of "dumping"; however, the pent up emotion is present and I wanted to show its controlling and pervasive effects.

The second part of the book revolves around unexpected modes of healing, and how these manifested slowly and quietly. Though I expected a clear and sudden change with a definitive stating: "I'm done", no such experience came to pass. Instead, Part II shows the slow seeping and gentle infiltration of change that quietly slipped into being. I began to experience I had will and that making peace with the past required discovering and using that will; the alternative kept me prisoner to outside events, people, or experiences (pleasant or difficult).

My aim in this book is to demonstrate that regardless of what life has dealt us in terms of experiences and challenges, we always have a choice concerning the manner in which we interpret events. I have offered two practices – psychosynthesis and the teachings of *A Course in Miracles* – to show a freeing alternative for understanding life's experiences. There are obviously many other practices and ways of seeing and understanding life. I share my own journey as a personal gift to you.

With many blessings on your life's journey,
Olivia

(1) Molly Young Brown, *Growing Whole*, Foreword
(2) For a clearer understanding of the difference between masculine and feminine qualities, see Mike Burke & Pierre Sarda, *Emergence des valeurs féminines dans l'entreprise, Une révolution en marche*

Preface: Setting the Stage

April 23, 2009

I awake terrified, shaken. In my nightmare, they (two men) are taking away children…where we don't know… A woman in our group of three (she, another man, and me) tries to stop them and has her head bashed in. I see her body taken away in a truck, the bashed head just protruding at the back.

As I write up the dream later I feel tense and scared…of what? I don't know. All is calm in my little house in the woods and I am safe, yet I have often felt afraid, petrified in my life. I have lived for years with an underlying current of fear, fear of *"not doing it right"*, somehow *"not being up to it"*. Not up to what? To <u>life</u>.

In my family we never spoke. We were not mute, but always on guard, like walking on eggs… treading carefully, oh so carefully. No one dared speak for him or herself, or go against the grain. I believe we were all afraid… I certainly was… afraid of a domineering, aggressive, angry father. Undoubtedly because of his own sense of personal failure, we children needed to fit a mold of perfection, a mold we never fit, no matter what we did.

My father hated disorder. Everything had to be clean, immaculate, and in its place; that included us. If you were somehow out of place there was *"hell to pay"* – shouting, hitting, threatening, criticizing, anything to make you fit some unknown, imagined image of perfection. My mother never intervened, except to cry, and plead: *"Stop An..!"* It didn't do much.

Unexpectedly, at the age of eight, I was sent to unknown grandparents in Chicago. Despite my childhood confusion and sadness at leaving my mother, those two years were wonderful, and another world was revealed to me. At 10, I returned to live with my parents. Life was again abusive, angry and totally irrational.

At thirteen, I returned to Chicago to live with my grandmother (my grandfather having died), but this time never to return to live with my parents. In terms of the world, I "grew up" at thirteen, but inside I remained a scared and frightened little girl. Since that time I have spent my life looking for something… a place to belong, someone to love me, care for me and take care of me, to take away the pain, and to "*fix it*".

As I already mentioned, in my family, we never spoke. I, faithful to family "rules", never spoke of anything related to my family's insular, strict ways of being. Traumatized, I ran away… to France, a country I lived in at age 11 when my mother was granted a teaching sabbatical. Though I have no particularly happy memories of that period, somehow France offered me an unconscious refuge or place of safety, and I felt I had to go there by hook or by crook. Today it is in rural, beautiful, quiet, Southwest France that I am writing… after all these years, finally saying something, though still aware of how carefully I weigh every word so as to avoid offence or upset. This programming was successfully drummed into me, and still today, though less intimidated and controlled, I feel its accusing, critically shaking finger of discontent.

Introduction: The Path of Love

In life we're all on the same path and ...we're all pursuing the same thing. This may sound absurd in today's world, which appears complex and diverse with different countries, languages, cultures, peoples, opportunities and choices. Yet, below the turbulent, often chaotic waves of change, new developments, findings and personal/family *"stories"*, we all seek the same thing. Deep within our being we seek connection and a need to matter to someone or something. Whether we call it a need for recognition, material success, status, friendship, power, whatever the term used, underneath our deepest desires and dreams, we're looking for love, an intangible state/quality and feeling that nourishes and sustains us and is indispensable to our existence.

In our world people can die of a broken heart... I've witnessed it. From a feeling of heart-shattering betrayal or abandonment, a break in connection, a person can give up the desire to live. Sometimes they emotionally retreat from life; sometimes they physically die.

Love **is** life giving. But, what exactly is it, and where does it come from? How do we find it? Despite our avid search, for the majority of us, through most of our lives (though interspersed with moments or periods of seeming love...) love remains just out of reach. Ram Dass (1) likens human beings to baby ducklings, mechanically following a mother duck. Hungry beings in search of a key that will open us to love, we mechanically follow whatever seems to open our hearts...always as if there were an outside key. When we believe we have found the answer and "fall in love", undoubtedly it does not last. It cannot last... nothing is this world is permanent. In the end, everything changes. In the end, we all die. But throughout life we remain like amoebas or parasites... never getting enough, always needing more, and living in constant fear that our life force – **love** – will forsake us...Maybe there is something we have misunderstood.

* * *

My own life experiences, though harsh as a child and at times seemingly hopeless, taught me that our true essence is love. The ultimate love is love of "Self", which presupposes the discovery or encounter with Self. Here is our life force, and it does not reside outside us. Only through a connection with Self can we experience true love and peace. And only by experiencing Self will we discover Truth, the truth about ourselves.

Author and psychosynthesis therapist, Piero Ferrucci, recounts a revealing story in his illuminating work, *What We May Be*. According to an ancient Eastern story, the gods *"concealed Truth inside the very heart of human beings. In this way they will look for it all over the Universe, without being aware of having it inside themselves all the time."*(2) Confused or misled, we look outside ourselves for sustenance and for love, and sever ourselves from "Self". In so doing, we cut ourselves off from the force of love and from our own truth… it is no wonder we shrivel and die, symbolically, then physically.

Something drives us though to maintain the search, like junkies in want of a next fix. We are spellbound by love… we talk and write about it, make films about it, and entertain myths and beliefs, hoping these will lead us to <u>true love</u>. The theme is universal: we continue blindly on the path of life, desperate beggars… grabbing, lying, and stealing… <u>for love</u>. Always seeking without, we are never satisfied and remain fearful of losing, not finding, or, being discovered undeserving and consequently forever cut off from love. If we would just stop long enough, look at this mental pattern or construct… look within… dare to question the preconceived notions of who we <u>think</u> we are, or who we have been <u>taught</u> we are, we might receive an inkling of what truly **is**…

* * *

The following narration is my "path of love". It is a passionate search for love, for "Self" with a capital "S", not the small concept of the self taught by the ego. My search was for permission <u>to exist</u>, as if that fact could be questioned. Yet, a small part of us (ego) keeps us drugged on guilt to the point we wonder if we even have the right to exist. Only "unreasonable love", *l'amour déraisonné*… love that could be termed "mad", "insane" and incomprehensible by the world according to the ego, allows us to look at life's events with another interpretation and realize that throughout all, "Self", and the overriding, ever present love of Self has always been there.

My story is one of trauma, loss, betrayal, pain, intermittent joy, anger, and eventually… slow discovery, opening, understanding, acceptance, and serenity. It is a story of love without reason, without explanation in terms of the world, but of awakening in terms of Spirit.

The story takes place in foreign lands and takes place "at home," deep within the Self. It is the story of a little girl who runs away across the ocean, far from family, far from what she knows, in order to create a new "self" in a new country with a new language, in the unconscious hope of finding a place where she can be accepted and loved.

For a while the attempt seemed to work, but life caught up and "catastrophe" hit… once, twice… enough to shake the belief in what so far had given my life meaning. I hit rock bottom. I could no longer understand or see how to advance; everything I had done seemed useless, a waste of life. As the Norma J. Morris Center's manual for "Adult Survivors of Child Abuse" describes, I hit a "breakthrough crisis" which pushed me to look at the repressed pain, anger and shame brought on by childhood abuse. (3)

Italian psychiatrist, Roberto Assagioli's, psychosynthesis (4) and the teachings of *A Course in Miracles* (5) "saved" me; these two approaches to life presented me with a new way to look at trauma, my pain, and the deep guilt I experienced within, similar to the indelible branding or marking of a slave. The inner work I embarked upon, using these tools and philosophy, allowed me to open to healing, after years of running. Running may help initially by removing you from a place of torture or abuse, but only looking within allows you to come to terms with life experiences… to see beneath the appearances and to offer healing.

I believe life repeatedly presents us with experiences to replay the script or lesson our healing requires, so we can see and feel (despite appearances) we have never been left or abandoned by Love. The message of psychosynthesis is love, the challenge to find love of Self. Reclaiming Self is a path of love, and psychosynthesis is a workable practice to reclaim or discover Self. For me, psychosynthesis also became the manual to further understand and apply the teachings of *A Course in Miracles*. Though the Course and psychosynthesis are distinct practices, they overlap and their messages are the same. The introduction to *A Course in Miracles* clearly states:

The course does not aim at teaching the meaning of love,

INTRODUCTION: THE PATH OF LOVE

for that is beyond what can be taught. It does aim, however, at removing the blocks to the awareness of love's presence, which is your natural inheritance. (ACIM introduction. Para.1.6-7)

No matter what our life's experiences, love has never been far away. Psychosynthesis reveals this to us as we discover the different parts of our selves, abandoned, discarded, traumatized, and uncared for over the years. In the end, **we** (and only we), using what Assagioli calls "will", open our hearts to the fragile, blustering, terrorized, aggressive, controlling, or shy aspects of our being and welcome them home, to love.

* * *

My story, this is my gift or invitation to journey within, to listen and find the symbolism in your own story… to uncover your own *"way of love"*. In this way, you will **know** deep within your being, when life seems most bleak, painful or impossible and without hope, healing is possible and around the corner.

A Course in Miracles, workbook lesson 31 reminds us:

"I am not the victim of the world I see." And lesson 193 teaches: *"All things are lessons God would have me learn."*

The Course teaches us that time's only purpose is to allow us to awaken from our "dream" of separation, hatred, and suffering; everything in our lives is to remind us to remember who we truly are. This is the aim of a journey to reclaim Self.

Releasing this "dream" or life drama may seem unattainable at times. As egos, we hold strongly to an unjust story of victimization, a belief in a *"dog eat dog"* world; yet this awakening is our only chance to find meaning in a chaotic, often unfriendly and violent world, where a dominant motivation is self-interest. Appearances must be deceiving. Things are not as they appear, and we must step back and look at events symbolically. *"Beware of seeing yourself mistreated,"* reminds the Course in chapter 27 entitled *"The Healing of the Dream".* And as Gandhi suggested, *"Be in the world what you want to see in the world."*

I believe (and I am not alone in voicing it) that our only hope for a sustainable world, for the protection of life – our own and that of our planet – in the face of abuse, devastation and selfish exploitation, is to *"change our minds"*, to *"see differently"* (6), to take responsibility for our own personal development, and to stop the infernal cycle of *"attack, defence, defence, attack."* As the Course maintains, it is the only way to peace.

* * *

P.S. This writing in no way attempts to present "Truth" or even "reality". As the founders and staff at the Option Institute in Sheffield, Massachusetts (7) suggest, what we believe about life is made up or "make-believe" – no one can prove it. What matters is how you decide to see things and how you decide to live accordingly. And if all beliefs are made up, why not make them up so they serve you, and make your journey more to your liking, not to your **ego's** liking, but to satisfy your deepest desires and aspirations? Many people will say: *"impossible, absurd,"* so I reply like the queen in Lewis Carroll's *Alice in Wonderland:*

> *I dare say, you haven't had much practice. When I was your age, I believed in at least half a dozen impossible things before breakfast.* (8)

What have you got to lose? You can always return to your initial, conditioned way of thinking at any time. What you believe and whether you live joyfully, or in fear and anger, is totally up to you.

---

(1) For an overview of Ram Dass's life in his own words, see Ram Dass § Mirabai Bush *Compassion in Action*
(2) Piero Ferrucci, *What We May Be*
(3) The Norma J Morris Center, www.ascasupport.org
(4) For a complete listing of works on Psychosynthesis, please see the bibliography.
(5) *A Course in Miracles*, (ACIM) Foundation for Inner Peace, 1996
(6) Cited in ACIM and title of the book *To See Differently* by Susan Trout
(7) The Option Institute, International Learning and Training Center, Sheffield, MA. www.option.org
(8) *Alice in Wonderland, and Through the Looking Glass*, by Lewis Carroll Wordsworth Editions 1993

Part I

CHAPTER 1

Crash Landing

It was Sunday morning, a perfect day: warm, dry and clear, blue sky with a few fluffy clouds. A. and I were to visit a house in the countryside, another possible rental, since we were not able to find a house for sale that suited both our tastes and needs. He thought we should build, and I was a bit sceptical since I knew how long that could take. After all, we lived in Southwest France where people knew how to enjoy life and take their time. This meant they had a non-linear, multi-tasked "juggling" approach to time, and one consequence was deadlines were fluid.

In the meantime, the little house we rented was not going to work long term; it was too damp and had little insulation, so was expensive to heat, and a bit noisy. We had just purchased a clothes dryer Saturday night, and instead of sleeping in lovingly this Sunday morning, cuddling and cosy in bed, A. had gotten up early to go "home" to get tools to install the dryer.

Hum, it's a bit of a long story. He was not divorced… and, there was no *official* separation. He and I had been together for a little over four years. We were one of many "illegitimate" couples in France. We had a house together and his wife lived in the family house, which he still frequented, particularly at lunchtime during the week, when it was her unspoken duty to prepare him lunch. This is France, and I lived in rural, beautiful, unpolluted, authentic France… "*la France profonde*" as the French describe it, "deep France". The well-known 19th century writer, Auguste Flaubert, depicts in his famous novel *Madame Bovary*, a clear and in many ways still valid, description of the ingrained, parochial attitudes of rural France.

A. and his wife worked together in his dental practice and though they were no longer romantically involved, they remained married and "*did not hate each other*" (as he repeatedly informed me); in France, a contract is a contract. Though it was not openly discussed, money was a central issue; A. risked losing everything (or close to everything) he had worked hard to earn if he tried to divorce and *Madame* refused. She had never worked (other than to assist him in his practice), had given him two children, and assisted him in building the practice. By law he would be obliged to *"keep her in the comfort to which she was accustomed"*, as well as give her the house, if he decided to leave. The long and the short of the story was, at the mature age of 56, A. would have little (if anything) to start a new life with his "*Dulcinea*" of four years, me.

Naturally, we had not spoken of these unpleasant details. In this part of the world, "*célà ne se fait pas.*" *(It's just not done.)* A. reassured me repeatedly he would be free, things would be fine, and of course, he loved me... or to use his own words: "*je t'adore*". *(I adore you.)* I trusted him, believed him, and loved him. We had lived through a number of ups and downs in our four and a half year relationship, and step-by-step, we had created a life together. Perhaps we only semi-lived together, since he returned home from time to time, particularly on workdays, but I also had a house from my previous married life about an hour's drive away.

I trusted him, his feelings, as well as my own, and what he told me. I felt he was the man I had always wanted and needed in life—cultured, debonair, attentive, intelligent, and devoted (in his own way). The difference in our situations was that **I** was divorced and alone, with no children; he on the other hand was married, had a neurotic and dependent wife, two adult boys to whom he was very attached, and I realize today, <u>no intention</u> of making waves within his 'tribe' and family. They had given him a kind of "permission" to live the way he was living, so unconsciously, in return, there was an understanding he was to be appreciative and fulfill family obligations. The whole set-up suited *Madame* entirely; she also had a lover, a married man with children.

This is a common state of affairs in France. Even former President Mitterand had a legal wife and official mistress... they were both present at his funeral. Only when things backfire, the unattached person usually gets hurt the most (as I was soon to learn). As to his *"permission"* (as they call it in French in the army), this is the word for "leave". *Madame* had in point of fact written me a long letter four years ago when I rejected A.'s declaration of affection (on the grounds that he was married). She had informed me how devastated and deflated he was, "*no longer the same man.*" In this letter, as well as in her quiet acceptance of the whole situation, A.'s wife acquiesced to his "leave", or "*permission*".

At the time of A.'s declaration of affection to me, we had known each other for two years as members of the same Argentinean tango association. Through dance we had become closer, and gotten to know each other during events and festivals. At one summer festival where we were dance partners, we found ourselves sharing the same bedroom (due to lack of availability). A. took advantage to confess his affections for me, and immediately made an avowal to his wife, who revealed in her letter, that *"de toute façon"* she had been aware of his feelings for me for some time and thought that I should be "honored," since in 28 years of marriage A. had never "faltered".

From my perspective her letter was an affirmation of a marriage that no longer worked, so I allowed myself to step in and follow my heart's desire. After consultation with a dear and "wise" woman-friend of eighty, I consented to explore this romantic relationship, since as my friend rightfully pointed out, there was no lying or deceit, and everything was out in the open and "known". On these terms we started to see each other four years ago. We did <u>fabulous</u> things together, spending our weekends walking in nature, dancing, or travelling in Europe and other lovely parts of France. We had similar interests, and felt very relaxed and at ease with one another. In no way did A. act like a married man; he was always available to do things or go away on weekends or longer vacations.

Spiritually we also seemed to be on a similar wavelength, and so nine months into the romantic phase of our relationship, I was well and truly, "in love". Perhaps you can understand my total confusion and devastation this sunny Sunday in early November 2006, when A., returning to our little house, looking sulky, grim and taciturn, suddenly metamorphosed into Mr. Hyde! Events then took a turn that dramatically changed my life.

My initial comment at a heavily hushed and grim breakfast table was that I did not want to be involved in his relationship with his wife (she had called totally enraged twice that very morning.) A's angry reply was: *"You should have said that ages ago."*

Sensing his anger, and my desire to avoid another argument, (we had been having a few recently) I remained quiet, and prepared to go outdoors into the resplendent day with my dog, Brownie. This brought on the response, that if I left, *"it was over…"*.

I went out nonetheless, feeling I needed to get away from the craziness. I had grown up in crazy, erratic behavior and anger as a child, and have always had an aversion for sudden and loud mood changes.

Imagine my confusion and hurt, when I returned an hour later, to a closed up, empty and silent house. A. had left, <u>never</u> to return… and what became harder for me to bear, never to give any explanation, other than **I** did not understand him or his situation. From his perspective, **I** was to blame.

The Wound

I felt devastated and totally destroyed. I couldn't stop crying. I sought help with a therapist, who said: *"you need help."* I had been vigilantly studying *A Course in Miracles* since my good friend and caring husband had changed <u>his</u> mind about marriage December 24th eight years ago. I read lessons entitled: *"God's Peace and Joy are mine."* Or, *"Let me be still and listen to the truth"(1),* to no avail. I found no truth and felt no peace, let alone joy. I was miserable, and totally destroyed.

I felt not only sadness, but also a sense of guilt that I *"should have seen"* A. did not really love me. When you love someone, you do not abandon, blame, and disappear; you "own" your stuff, even if it is difficult. So I kept waiting and nothing came – only silence. Then the anger started to boil. I woke up in the night realizing what "is", or what had always been: it had always been about <u>him,</u> <u>for</u> him. As long as I did what he liked/wanted, then he "loved" me. And today, I was abandoned. I had no relationship, and after several months, began to realize I never had one.

It was like a drug or a drunk wearing off; the feeling was horrendous, and I felt I would not survive. I felt there was nothing left of me. I had been so "screwed!" And this was not the first time… What made this betrayal so hard to bear, was the reminiscence of my husband walking out after 12 years of marriage. And deeper in my past was the distant memory of the first 13 years of my life, spent in a violent, degrading, harshly critical and totally closed family environment. I preferred not to remember.

I read, continued therapy, listened to numerous tapes on love addictions, and studied what the Course refers to as "Special Relationships". The more I read the more I could not believe what was said, and the more devastated I felt.

I thought I was intelligent. I was a life coach, had worked in personal development and communication training in companies in Europe for 15 years! I had been successful and happy. Two years ago (at A's suggestion), I had started a life coaching practice using our house as a base. I worked with clients by phone, from my little house in the woods, and from our place together. Though many people in the area told me this was not the *"pays de coaching",* I had started to develop a small practice and I enjoyed my work.

How could I have been so blind vis à vis A? My own guilt trip increased my pain and the debilitating burden I felt. Over the months to come I tried to cover up my pain, continued with on-going clients, then slowly, quietly, let my work dissolve, until I closed down my practice one year later. I was unable to accompany and help people in their pain when I was devastated, empty, and bleeding. For the first time in my life, I felt absolutely bereft inside, betrayed and utterly confused, since I had not seen catastrophe coming. I had survived a violent, unstructured family life, I believed, due to my own inner guidance and resources, and in this relationship I had felt **so** sure about A. I had been so happy, yet look how he had betrayed me! I could no longer accompany others; I no longer trusted myself, felt like a fake, and could not go on. It was obvious I needed time for my own healing.

(1) ACIM Workbook lessons 105 and 106

CHAPTER 2

Psychosynthesis

Psychosynthesis was a lifesaver. I'll forego the details concerning how I stumbled upon it; suffice it to say I had been introduced to John Whitmore's book on *Coaching and Performance* through my management training. In turn, this led me to his wife, Diana Whitmore and her book on *Psychosynthesis Counseling in Action. (1)*

I was fascinated with the approach. I started to search, digging desperately for psychosynthesis training, like a dog urgently seeking a buried bone. As a result, in January 2007, 6 weeks after A. walked out, I left for a weeklong exploration and training at The Psychosynthesis and Education Trust in London, a center founded by Dr. Roberto Assagioli himself in 1974. That week and the London Trust, were a real godsend... a coming home, and the beginning of healing.

Unfortunately, living in France with no income (due to closing my practice), I was unable to finance training and study with this professional organization in London. I needed to branch out and discover a way to continue my healing work without regular trips to the U.K., or even Paris. In my searching I was fortunate to stumble upon Molly Young Brown's online training and coaching practice! (2)

I was familiar with Molly's work from her books, and knew that she had worked directly with Assagioli before his death, so I lost no time in speaking with her on the phone. In short order I took the plunge and signed up for a 12 module on-line, intensive training in *Personal and Spiritual Psychosynthesis.* This was the beginning of an in-depth exploration of unknown, forgotten, traumatic experiences of my life. The work did not go as fast as a part of me would have liked, but continued, opened and exposed (like an onion) layer after layer of repressed fear, guilt, pain, and eventually anger.

In mid September 2007 as part of a module entitled *Working with my demons/Discovering my survival personalities,* I wrote:

> For over a month I have been aware of an incredible fear within, a fear to step out, fear to fail, or a feeling I will die... an inability to walk away and forget A. I am still suffering (though he is out of my life).
>
> I have been listening and re-listening to a Caroline Myss

series of CD's entitled The Call To Live A Symbolic Life (3). *I can see a symbolic reason to my pain and past suffering, a 'contract' with A. so to speak... Yes, I feel we had business together, though I cannot totally integrate this idea; still the pain comes in convulsions, emotional paralysis and crying.*

The Firman and Gila (4) book, Psychosynthesis: A Psychology of the Spirit *is a lifesaver and helps me validate what I experienced and feel today, so as not to believe I am crazy. It helps me to put my finger on behavior I want to change, but can't seem to; my repeated reaction seems to be in the cells, deep within... no matter how illogical, unhelpful, masochistic or crazy, one part of me seems to shout.*

Trying to work on the level of outer changes in my life, I want to leave, but there is much to do and organize to close out a life of 18 years in France. I have so little strength... some days just waking up, washing, eating, grocery shopping, looking for work, writing business letters, swimming or walking with Brownie, is all I can do. Then of course there is reading: A Course in Miracles, A Psychology of Spirit, Non violent Communication-*Marshall Rosenberg, Caroline Myss... then, writing, meditating, allowing the visualizations, writing to "Self"... trying to find my own support within and praying...*

*I am seeing so much stuff going on in a buried part of my being... I feel my sense of I/Self is faulty, not able to be present with all of the horrible stuff... What do I **do** with all this pain and fear?*

* * *

One day, after going deeply into an exercise entitled, *"What's the longing in me, what am I afraid of?"* I allowed myself to experience the deep fear brought up by this meditation or inner contemplative exercise.

Unexpectedly, I had the awareness of a young, blackened woman living in the bowels of a ship, the engine room. She lurks among the machinery. It's hot and greasy, noisy from machinery... she's filthy, her hair stringy and black from grease and oil. They throw her old, disgusting food from time to time. She seems to keep the ship moving, but never comes out, never sees or speaks to anyone, never comes up to the light of day. Her skin is yellowish; she hides among the machinery. The noise is deafening... somehow I know she is used for sex, but solely to assuage a man's impulse, for she is not beautiful or desirable.

I am <u>stunned</u>, floored. There is no fresh air in her world. No one cares about her, yet the ship would not advance without her and the work she does in the engine room, she who never breathes the clean ocean air, nor sees the wide expanse of blue sea and sky. I feel I cannot leave her, but she is **terrified** to come out. My throat is dry and I feel stunned beyond belief...

She is not chained to anything, but hides and runs when I try to approach. She would be so dazzled/blinded by the light. I ask her gently not to go, and stroke her greasy cheek. I am numbed, gob smacked, and somehow I know there is more... to the left, hidden under an enormous machine is a filthy, black blanket with a dead baby in it. The baby has been cold and stiff for ages. (How strange... I never had children because deep within me I was afraid of the black dead muck I would bring into the world).

As I sit with this vision, it feels horrible, so very sad, and dreadful; I cannot find words to describe my incredulity. The name "Esther" comes to me for this wordless, terrified, dirty woman forgotten in the bowels of the ship. I take her with me and bathe her. For the first time she has a warm bath, and is clean. She eats warm and fresh food, but does not say a word.

What are her needs? (This is a question from the psychosynthesis exercise). The answer comes easily: <u>recognition, caring, love, help to come out</u>.

A few days later we go on the deck together, walk and drink hot chocolate in a lounge chair, and sit. Esther never says a word. The ship moves quietly across the ocean. Later, I know we have to do something with the dead baby she carries. I cannot just throw it into the sea – I just can't. Then the image of a funeral at the stern of the big ship comes: a cremation in a large Moroccan "tagine" or earthenware container. As I gently throw the large ashes onto the sea, they instantly turn into soft down feathers carried by the wind. Gulls, following the ship, collect them before they fall to make soft nests for their babies.

Life feels softer, and Esther looks relieved. She walks the deck alone now, wearing a flowing, cream-colored linen outfit *from the 1920's with a hat. Her look is serene and clear, but still she does not speak. I can feel the ocean liner crossing the wide expanse of sea with Esther walking the deck. I have no idea where it is going, and neither does she. At times she seems serene with not knowing, and merely being in the ocean breeze, walking, and looking at the blue horizon.*

Perhaps this experience corresponded with me feeling O.K. doing nothing, with my solitude and with the "death" of my life as I had envisaged it. 'Allowing' and **faith** became qualities I wanted to develop. In any case, this experience based on work with Molly shortly into my psychosynthesis exploration, was surreal for me, but reflected much I had hidden and fled from in my life. I guess it was time for it to surface.

---

(1) J. Whitmore *Coaching for Performance*, & D. Whitmore *Psychosynthesis Counselling in Action*
(2) See InterMountain Psychosynthesis Center, Mt Shasta, CA.
    http://www.mollyybrown.com for information on online training and guiding
(3) See http://www.myss.com for a complete list of Caroline Myss's works and CD's
(4) J Firman and A. Gila, *Psychosynthesis: A Psychology of the Spirit*

Exploring Psychosynthesis

As part of my training in psychosynthesis I was assigned to read the book, *What We May Be* by Piero Ferrucci, student and close disciple of Roberto Assagioli. The title of his work was promising, and Ferrucci's statements about *"the self not being some state located out there, which we must look for and strive hard to reach"* was comforting, and reassuring. He affirmed: *"we already are the self all the time"*. (1) His words were heartening but perplexing... I experienced very little sense of "self". I seemed to have totally imploded and no longer felt I existed without A. What was this elusive "self" that Ferrucci referred to... strong and indestructible like a diamond?

Lia's story in his chapter *"Totally Immeasurable"* fully resonated in truth for me; she described the need for other people's input in order to exist. She explained:

I needed other people's judgment in order to convince myself that I existed... I feel this sense of neglect, of uselessness, the way you feel when there is nothing you can do. One builds an airplane and then leaves it there to collect cobwebs. One exists, but the whole world is too busy to take notice.

I feel a sense of torment. One asks why, with despair. Nobody knows that the airplane exists. **Something happened, but nobody knows about it.** *(2)*

This experience and fear felt true for me. In my early reports to Molly, I wrote:

Something will happen, but no one will know about it. That has been my haunting fear since adolescence if I were not in a relationship with a man. I felt, or was terrified that I JUST DID NOT EXIST if not cared for, thought about, and validated by a relationship with a man.

I had never been aware of this devouring need. Popular enough, and picky about the men I dated over the years, I was quite proud I had waited as long as I had to find the "right" marriage partner, someone intelligent and kind, with whom I had good rapport. But now I could feel the power behind the unconscious imperative to be with a man, and I decided to impose a difficult, but self-imposed period of solitude. The following comes from my journal during this time:

> *Yes, self-reliance has been a consequence of the past six weeks; I am almost totally alone, without a relationship or the hope of one. Ferrucci speaks of this crucial fact of existence: <u>basic aloneness</u>. I have spent my whole life running from, hiding, and closing my eyes to this fact.*
>
> *Is it a fact? I cannot bear it: I am <u>terrified</u>. Yes, I expected the environment; i.e. my entourage to supply me with what I illusorily (?) believed not to have: <u>strength, direction, even life itself</u>."* (Refer to Ferrucci, chapter 5 p.69)

Sad as it may be to confess, I often felt no direction and no real life without an intimate relationship with a man, so the following words come as no surprise:

> *This period of time since A. left has been a real test, a true confronting of demons for me. What if Ferrucci is mistaken? And **I** have no self? It somehow got forgotten in the mixture, or left out…*

This possibility did not at all seem unlikely to me since my father had joked for years about finding me in a garbage can, and a part of me wondered if it were not true. I must have been faulty and have been thrown away. If not, why would my father shout at me for everything, hit me, and never like anything I did?

Intense fear of "no self" is only one consequence of child abuse on adult life. For a fuller understanding and explanation of lasting consequences on one's adult life, as well as help in healing from these soul-shattering wounds, the Norma J. Morris Center in California is a vital resource. (3)

Subpersonalities

After several months into psychosynthesis work, through reading, meditation and free drawing, I started working with what Assagioli called "subpersonalities." I equate these to Jung's archetypes and the work of Caroline Myss (4), and in French jargon what I now refer to as *"ma famille nombreuse"* (my big/numerous family).

I wrote in one of my reports to Molly:

> *I have become very clear on two subpersonalities who hate each other and are at war. In my free drawing there is a*

handcuffed young woman lying face down... waiting for the next attack. She has a respite from time to time, but is afraid, terrified of the next blow... not daring to stand up, and not knowing how to get away. There is someone else, an Amazon-like female figure in my drawing, beating up the small fragile creature on the floor, who doesn't understand, and who hurts... This strong figure has become clearer to me now (with the help of the Firman and Gila book). She's the queen in Alice and Wonderland *(!) "Off with her head!"*

Goodness! I never knew **she** *existed. She reflects the characteristics A. complained about in me as too "yang", not gentle or feminine... In any case, she is impatient and knows what she wants in her kingdom – that little helpless waif, the one she beats up on, is not welcome!*

Dialoguing with subpersonalities:
(Exercise from Molly Y. Brown's *Growing Whole*). The following is a response to what each subpersonality has to say, and what it needs.

a) What the wounded part of me has to say:
I'm so afraid, stepped on, apparently horrible, ugly, and always wrong... My role is to be beat up, hit, spit upon, degraded, dumped on... I'm so tired and worn out, always trying to "get it right". I never do, so I get beat up again.

I feel like I'm tied to A... and he can smack me around. I have a black eye, yet I'm supposed to look "mignonne" (cute and sweet) and pretty... I'm so afraid to go places alone in case I faint... or die... so I hang on to him. (Before him there was S., and before him, my husband. I have <u>always</u> been accompanied).

Often, I just want to die; I want it all to stop. I feel lost, so confused, and can't see my way out. So it goes around, around and around, getting battered, beaten, insulted, raped (if they want), <u>used</u>... used so <u>they</u> can look good or feel O.K.

I'm worn out, pale, thin, and without center or depth to draw upon. I feel empty, drained, sad and afraid. I see no way out because I don't have strength and if I ask for change I get hit harder.

The aggressive "yang" female entity looks back with disdain, disgust, and derision. She is cloaked in a puritanical lady-like garb, a bit like Queen Victoria… She is definitely the *"off with her head"* queen depicted in Lewis Carroll's *Alice in Wonderland*. She hates this insipid creature who whines and wimps around and says:

> *For God's sake, get a life… who are you kidding? You're still whining and slinking around at <u>your</u> age? <u>When</u> will you grow up? He's an asshole – just drop him! Do something else!*
>
> *I'm bright, intelligent, and need to be recognized for my abilities. Stop dragging me down and acting like a spoiled brat! For God's sake, I want to get on with life… do, create, learn, and <u>she</u> just holds us back and keeps sapping the energy.*
>
> *GET RID OF HER! Get her out of this story. We don't want her. She's stupid, insipid and ugly. GROW UP! She's messing up my life; I was supposed to do things, be recognized, and be somebody. She's messing it up. Life was not supposed to look like this. Who needs her? Get her out of here <u>now</u>!*

Goodness, what energy! This part of me is definitely at war with the scared, frightened, wounded part. These two parts of me, both survival personalities, had pushed me along in life despite my confusion and fear, particularly the 'Queen.' Both were in need of great understanding, compassion and love (especially the terrified inner child I refer to as 'waif'). This internal battle reflected an unconscious assimilation of the hostile, critical "executioner" I had grown up with, which a part of me continued to need, believing I indeed **was** wrong and bad to bury the anger that otherwise would have exploded to the surface.

> *I became aware of another hidden part of my being, particularly when I listened to quiet music. She was "the dancer," graceful, lithe, slender, supple, and sensitive. I went to a tango workshop last week and one class was free dance expression; I felt happy to let her go, and express herself. <u>I experienced total bliss.</u>*
>
> *This dancer subpersonality was also never allowed expression when I was a child. Music and dance were taboo, a waste of time according to my father. Despite my first grade teacher's report, which wrote what a talented singer I was, suggesting I*

develop my voice, I was never allowed to follow that route. My father was livid when he read that report card… I hate to think what he said to the teacher.

The less energetic and vocal member of the "family" I call my "waif". I encountered her for the first time during an early exercise at the Psychosynthesis Trust in London. She seemed often to appear in tandem with the aggressive self-loathing aspect of myself, which was yet to manifest clearly as the violent "queen". I always associated the violent, hating energy in my life with my father and his multi-faceted abusive behavior. As a child I had been subjected to regular shouting, psychological belittlement, and physical slapping, hair pulling, and hitting. I never did anything right, and only served to clean the house, or to sit quietly out of sight, without making a sound. I was not allowed toys, friends, or to go out unaccompanied. When I was ten, things progressed to sexually serving my father after school; and when I was eleven, I remember being forced to clean, and re-clean the balcony railing from our apartment overlooking the Pacific Ocean in California. Sadly, in the year we lived there, I was never allowed to set foot on the beach.

My horror was intense when I realized I had internalized and turned against myself the harsh, hateful and critical demoralization I had grown up with. It manifested as the *"off with her head"* Queen who despised the fearful, self-effacing waif, and actually wanted to destroy her. I learned later in my training that it is quite common to have subpersonalities in conflict, greatly draining life force, but also drawing attention to a debilitating blockage in personal development.

(1) Piero Ferrucci, *What We May Be*, chapter 5 p. 67
(2) Piero Ferrucci, *What We May Be*, quotations from chapter 5, "Totally Immeasurable" (P.69)
(3) Norma J Morris Center and ASCA (Adult Survivors of Child Abuse) www.ascasupport.org
(4) Caroline Myss, *Sacred Contracts*

My Survival Personalities

July 5th, 2007

About 3 months into psychosynthesis work, I was spending a quiet, rather lonely summer when I wrote:

I cannot put Psychosynthesis: A Psychology of the Spirit *down. It feels like finally coming home, and resonates with something lost or far away in me. It's like I've known something before, all along… puts many pieces into a puzzle I could not work out.*

This resounding personal truth started with the introduction to the book, where the authors describe Roberto Assagioli as a psychoanalytic "heretic" refusing to accept Freud's reductionism and neglect of the positive dimensions of human personality.

I felt a type of 'thank you' as if someone, "heretic" or not, knew and explained my experience, gave me a path and a way out. Thank God, we are more than just our pathologies.

No one ever spoke about what went on in our house. No one ever <u>came</u> to our house: no stranger was allowed. To this day, I believe my ex-husband is the only outsider to have set foot within my parents' home. My sister never dated. We never had friends, and my mother had no social life. Amazing what a life fear begets!

When I was 10 years old a boy from my class somehow got my phone number and called the house. I got a 'whacking' you would not want to know about. No one ever went against Daddy's wishes without paying, and we all acquiesced, because we were afraid, and thought the behavior was 'normal.' Nothing was ever said <u>about anything</u>. My father did not work, so was always present to be sure you did what you were "supposed to." If you were expected home from school at 3:15 p.m. (it took 15 minutes to walk), you'd better be there at 3:15 sharp.

* * *

At the age of thirteen I was fortunate to be sent a second time to live with my grandmother in Chicago. Though no one explained the reason I was initially sent to my grandparents at the age of eight, I see today that this foster care greatly contributed to my development and allowed me to experience another way of life, and know there was a way out. I worked hard in high school and got top grades. Education and scholarships became my unconscious passport to freedom. At 16, when unexpected events almost sent me back to the lion's den, I ended up becoming a precocious undergraduate freshman at the University of Chicago.

While at the university I became interested in boys, but would experience panic attacks and great manic mood swings when things became intimate. I tried to see a therapist at the University Health Clinic. When I started describing events from my family, the therapist showed interest as if he had a "real live case" sitting in his office; his energy changed as he looked out over his glasses at me. I felt like a rat in a cage. I ran away after one session and never went back. I didn't want to be "a real live case." His look and that experience made me feel exactly what my father repeated over and over again: "not good enough, deficient, incapable, weird, bad." I never tried therapy again; instead I read books and alone tried to understand, change, and adjust.

* * *

When my husband and I broke up in 1999/2000 after twelve years of marriage – a time of relative peace and comfort in my life – I experienced incredible pain, panic and a sense of profound abandonment and unworthiness. Deeply depressed and afraid, I turned to *A Course in Miracles*, a self-study spiritual course, which offered an explanation of toxic relationship dynamics and an alternative belief system. Though appealing, these beliefs seemed impossible to put into practice. Similar to life in general, I felt I was missing the "How to" guide for ingrained, stubborn, or plain inept dummies... I continued to perpetrate the abuse by incriminating my inability to change my attitudes.

But now, after all these years I found something that rang true in my own personal experience... not what I **wanted** to experience, what I had experienced. I wrote in my work for Molly:

Today and last night, the more I read of Psychosynthesis: A Psychology of the Spirit, *the more I feel an emerging key, like a dim light...(though I can't believe it).*

Finally, there exists "an approach firmly rooted in Western psychology, yet consistent with widely disparate traditions" (A Psychology of the Spirit, *chapter 1 p. 16) For me who has experimented with a mishmash of different traditions, never experiencing true affinity to any one, it's like being welcomed and accepted; finally, being OK, just perhaps. And, it gives me a key to open and apply some of the exercises in the Course as well!*

The explanation of Assagioli's Egg model [I had discovered this model at The Psychosynthesis and Education Trust in London during the Essentials program] *somehow puts my experience in 3-D and gives the perfect link between "I" and "Self". In other words I sense the possibility of a link to something greater than myself, something greater than my pain and my experiences in life. This is a really eye opening possibility for me.*

Roberto Assagioli in his famous Egg diagram or model of the individual, speaks of the "I" or the "personal self". In his model we discover both a passive element and observing quality of the self, and an active agent, or "will-er." Molly Young Brown explains that:

As we identify ourselves more closely with the personal self, the "I", we may feel or sense an even deeper identity, a spiritual Source within us and encompassing us. In psychosynthesis and in other transpersonal psychologies, this underlying mysterious Presence is called Self, or Higher Self. (1)

"Self" with a capital "S", as Firman and Gila explain, *"is not represented at all* (in the diagram) *and should be imagined as pervading all of the areas of the diagram and beyond."(2)* Brown explains: *"Self transcends our personality, our situation in life, our roles, our gender. Yet Self is present no matter how confused, in pain, or lost we may feel."(3)*

Here I felt a trace of hope, real hope… something existed outside the realm of incomprehensible acts, pain and horror. I continued in my writing:

*Then there is the "crème de la crème": primal wounding, what Firman and Gila call stage zero: <u>Survival</u>! To survive, we become objects, not individuals, and create a survival personality. The authors explain that we seek to "separate from consciousness the shame, helplessness, isolation, anxiety, abandonment… **and** the ability to love, trust, connect with the Divine, hiding the gifts as well as the pain…"(1) It feels like* someone has given me the right to relax and know I'm part of the human race, not different and weird.

Firman and Gila speak of "an internalised pattern resulting from the non-empathetic environment."(1) How true! I flipped out in the Essentials training in London when I saw that **I** was continuing abuse, criticism and hatred in my life... Today I was long gone from my father and frightening childhood environment... I no longer needed to fear being forced to return as I had for many years – from 12-21 years old. Still, somehow I could not be kind, understanding and gentle with myself. I was afraid deep down that something was wrong with me. I must be crazy... **why would anyone who had lived through what I did, perpetuate that suffering?**

I continued to write, in relief:

So I'm not stupid, crazy, and a total moron. <u>I survived</u> as my therapist has repeated many times. I have always belittled this fact by thinking: "yeah – so what? Look what a mess of it I've made. I can't let go and be happy. I get anxious over ludicrous things: dirt, disorder, and messed up bathrooms with wet towels badly (or not) hung up."

As a child, when things were out of order, Daddy beat the shit out of me. Even if I was in the process of having a shower, he could come in unexpectedly and slap me across the face with my wet washcloth because the bathroom wasn't glimmering, clean and shiny; there would be mist from using hot water, and a bathmat on the floor...

But, that's over now. I don't live there anymore. Why do **I** flip out, especially when A. became angry if I dared to ask him to hang up his towel, and leave mine fresh so I could benefit from a dry, cosy towel when it's cold outside and I need to hurry to work? Besides... **I** did all the cleaning and washing anyway!

Perhaps, it is pretty neat what I did to survive. The realization has started to seep in. Today, I thought: "I done good" as my mother used to say. It's not my fault, and I'm doing O.K. I've been at stage zero my entire life... and it's fabulous!

I see my free drawing from the other day in a different light. It shows a coming out of a long, dark tunnel. There's a lake – I love to swim, and adore water – water always reflected safety *and refuge for me. There is also a unicorn, a magical, masculine energy I've recently imagined, who is smiling. Up to the left there is an angel or some benevolent spirit, and gentleness. All around grows long sweet, green grass (what the French call "fat" grass i.e. lush), and a sweet innocent little bunny rabbit is nibbling in the grass, unafraid, and not running...*

Firman and Gila write: "*Survival personality is fundamentally a broken empathy with ourselves.*" (4)

Do you mean I actually had empathy for myself? What a thought... I always felt so cut off from myself... I could see and feel pain in others and couldn't bear it, but didn't dare go inside to feel my own pain... I just wanted to "get on with life."

I have finally started to allow the feelings to surface, instead of running away... and perhaps I can discover compassion for <u>me</u>... what an incredible possibility! I'm at Stage One exploring this possibility. I am still hearing the berating, judgmental voices, but I'm hanging in there, and doing something for myself I never could have thought possible. I am finally out of the tunnel and exploring the light. (As well as the tunnel)

And there is the promise of discovering my **authentic self***, who I really am! All thanks to 'Papa Assagioli'. The war is over, and I did survive, perhaps not too badly after all. (Smile)*

* * *

Deeper exploration and realizations included the following comments:

As I have already said the Firman and Gila book has been a lifesaver, like a long sought-after key into the rusted, forgotten, impenetrable lock of my survival personalities. I am discovering the reason I cannot let go of the horrific pain and suffering concerning first A. – a partner I could see was unhealthy for me – and secondly, my father. Despite the life-threatening behavior this latter subjected me to...despite everything, I could not be angry with him.

I can see now how I have internalised abuse and criticism to the detriment of self-compassion. I have always pushed myself, and never felt I was good enough... When I first realized this in

London, it almost sent me over the edge... What do I do now? There's no hope of escape if the executioner is inside you!

When I read in *Psychosynthesis: A Psychology of Spirit* on page 163:

> I have been so traumatized by significant others that I have been left feeling I am a worthless, bad person. I feel I am a failure and have no right to be alive, I hate myself, I'm simply wasting space on the planet.

I felt I could have written those words. They adequately express what Esther has felt and could not face.

Firman and Gila go on to say in their book:

> In some ways, though, I feel like by accepting this painful identity I am maintaining a meaningful loyal connection to my significant others; in other ways this identity is a way of holding my trauma in the hope that the truth of it may finally be seen and validated. (5)

In my comments I write:
> I feel the shock of absolute truth. No wonder I couldn't throw away Esther's dead baby, and no wonder I hang on to my pain. I have been protecting my father and mother my entire life, while also hoping against hope somehow, someone would know what happened and understand the deep pain I experience and keep hidden inside.
> My parents would not accept or <u>hear</u> anything I ever tried to say about the past or my pain. Whatever I tried fell on deaf ears, or they somehow showed I disrupted things. Always I have felt at fault, as if my mere presence... as if I hadn't been there, things would have been O.K. Even today, through silence, they ignore me and seem to forget I exist.
> How I needed validation, someone who could understand and recognize my quiet suffering, my inability to change things. This validation would have granted a " right to exist". But my deep desires always fell on deaf ears, right down to A. who was incapable of recognizing how hurtful his actions were. Instead

the problem in the relationship was always my fault, and he walked out to make me suffer, to punish "the bad girl".

*I am beginning to see... like looking through a dirty, encrusted windowpane... the depth of abuse I lived through, never realizing the extent to which my mother was also responsible... for doing nothing. Still, somehow I cannot **really** hear it. Perhaps I don't want to. As a child, my mother was my only hope in life, though she did nothing but cry.*

As I become aware of these points, I feel weak, hurt, in pain and bleeding... The internalised executioner, my queen subpersonality shouts to "get on with life" and " stop harping on the past." She is not alone. I feel the presence of another cold, critical "relation": a controlled, small, strong and ruthless South American Indian. He reflects the great resistance to opening the door of my remembering and looking within. This South American Indian has a painted face and feathers in his hair. I believe he can take life in an instant, without flinching... if the rules are broken. He does not react to pain or blood and is ruthless to ensure rules are followed!

I see a parallel with my sister who lives by strict rules. She certainly followed Daddy's rules and became a first-rate lawyer, and later was attracted to a spiritual practice with stringent principles. Unlike myself, she has repeatedly been able to inflict incredible discipline and pain on herself through diet, exercise, and work. There is a second parallel in the appearance of this new subpersonality: my father is South American, of Indian extraction. And I, I felt unable to break the rules of silence; never say a word to anyone about anything that happened. **NEVER.**

(1) Molly Y. Brown, *Growing Whole*, chapter 3, p. 41
(2) Firman & Gila, *Psychosynthesis: A Psychology of the Spirit*, p. 20
(3) Growing Whole, chapter 3, p. 41
(4) Firman and Gila, *Psychosynthesis: A Psychology of the Spirit*, p. 49
(5) Ibid. p. 163

CHAPTER 3

The Guardian*

This morning I held my little Brownie in love… or maybe he held me. Despite his size, he is the largest container of love, acceptance and joy I have ever witnessed (next to his "sister" Misty, who died 12 years ago). He is the incarnation of the bigger-than-life, orange '*Cuddly Dudley*' toy dog I so craved when I was eight years old. Cuddly Dudley had soulful eyes and long silky ears; Brownie has dark, deep eyes filled with love, compassion, understanding and playfulness. When I adopted him in 1998 at Christmas in Paris, he did not resemble who he is today. He was skinny, almost fur-less (shaven) and ugly… He looked like he had been in a concentration camp. Despite his looks and the other 499 dogs available for adoption, he exuded a calm knowing and acceptance that caught my attention.

Over ten years later, I have held Brownie in love and respect and he has returned it tenfold. To be exact, he has been my 'guardian' all these years. Two weeks after I adopted him, my husband walked out… needed time "to find himself." Though I tried to be understanding and patient, a year and a half later we decided to divorce. It was a horrific shock, for though I had felt for a number of years that B. was not stable and at peace deep down, I always believed or was confident that with understanding and time, he would find himself and be happy. Alas, that was not the case.

When I was a child, I needed someone to play with and love me unconditionally, protect and comfort me. It took me years to see how totally lost and left to my own devices I actually was as a child. My parents may have been my progenitors but they were in no way ready or able to be true guardians or parents. I was left alone, criticized or shouted at, hit, used, and abused. By the age of thirteen, luckily, I left home and went to live far away with my grandmother. I never returned.

My first experience away from my parents happened unexpectedly when I was eight years old. I was sent (without warning or explanation) to live with my grandparents in Chicago. They lived in a 14-room, dark, forbidding house in the inner city… at the time, a poor portion of town.

Though my grandmother was extremely agile for her age (75), my grandfather was weak and in poor health. I was put into his mother's (my great grandmother's) big, heavy front room, a room furnished with French antiques, cactus-like plants, and a stuffiness that revealed a desire to keep things as they were in an attempt to respect the past and those who have gone before.

I remember lying in the big double bed at night feeling alone, afraid of the shadows created by the cacti and the light from the street. To lessen the fear and terror I felt, I imagined the bed was a spaceship with a dome that would close up to protect Cuddly Dudley and me from the heaviness, loneliness, and foreboding I experienced. Today I can see that Brownie is the incarnation of that 'Cuddly Dudley' I so longed for and needed when I was eight. I am amazed to have manifested in flesh and blood the living version of my 8-year-old stuffed canine companion!

Brownie has been and **is** an amazing guardian and manifestation of love. He has taken care of me through the pain of my divorce, and through an even more painful separation with a man I loved two years ago. Through Brownie I am held in love. He has always been there and never abandoned me.

Patterns and Conditioning

When I was ten years old I returned to live with my parents, and life presented me with incomprehensible experiences of neglect, physical, emotional, and sexual abuse. These experiences and hateful messages permeated my being, leaving deep scars of fear, lack of trust, a sense I did not deserve goodness, and worse, a sense I did not deserve to exist. My father used to joke about finding me in a garbage can. Whatever I did, said, or did not do, was ALWAYS wrong.

I was fortunate to return to live with my grandmother at age 12 (my grandfather died when I was 10). Still, life became a challenge of survival, pleasing others, and taking care of them, so **I** could exist. I was taken care of, though love was not evident or visible. *"You had to work hard to deserve."* I successfully worked my way (mostly due to scholarships) through high school, college, and graduate school, but always feeling a deep sense of not belonging or being fundamentally different and undeserving. Some internal force however, pushed me along in life, and pushed me to follow a dream to go to France. I succeeded in doing graduate work in Paris, and found a job with a company that legally introduced me through official administrative channels, making a non-European Union student into a worker, something the French immigration officials informed me was impossible.

Adult life presented me professional success and a pleasant, often fun though unstable, 12-year marriage with B, an Australian I met in graduate school. Despite these positive turns of events, the uncomfortable feeling of being a misfit never left me, and I continued to experience incredible anxiety when I went into totally unknown situations. In time, two major emotional break-ups and abandonment (first my marriage, then a four-year affair with A, a man I adored) brought me to my knees and pushed me to open the cobwebbed doors and hidden recesses to confront family conditioning and repressed pain in my unconscious mind.

The fear to look within was enormous – I so wanted to erase the pain and the past as if it had never happened (and I might add, so did everyone in the family). The denial over the years had been and still is, mammoth. But for me the personal pain was too much. With the help of a psychologist and my own discovery of psychosynthesis (as well as other tools), I started to unfold and look at the destructive, criminal story of abuse and neglect.

The journey has been hard, full of previously unshed tears and heart-wrenching anguish. But through it all, Brownie has been there, always knowing when to cuddle close to me or jump into my lap. His head is wet with tears, but steadfast he remains; no pain is too great for him to hold and accompany. During this period of healing, people have come and gone in my life; they also have their pain and suffering and often want to push it down so they can "get on with life." I have also reacted in this way, but have discovered the truth in the adage: *"the only way through, is through"*. At some point it is time to confront and make peace with your own story.

This time of great aloneness (other than Brownie), personal discovery, and healing has allowed me to open my eyes and see all the love, support and caring that come my way... in ways and forms I do not suspect... in four-footed canine companions, or in last-minute synchronistic occurrences dealing with my health or financial situation.

> *A Course in Miracles tells us in several of its lessons:*
> *God's Will for you is perfect happiness... joy is our function here... let us try to find that joy that proves to us and all*

the world God's Will for us. It is your function that you find it here, and that you find it now. For this you came. (1)

How hard it is to see joy at times. Then I look at Brownie, always able to remember joy, the present moment, and acceptance of what life brings, for he too is now being brought lessons of ill health and physical pain. And I realize what a teacher and lover I have.

Unshaken does the Holy Spirit look on what you see; on sin and pain and death, on grief and separation and on loss. Yet does He know one thing must still be true; God is still Love, and this is not his Will. (2)

The lessons in our life are not easy to understand, let alone forgive, but somehow, somewhere, if we look deeply, there is a love, a presence, "being taken care of." It's a deep feeling, often difficult to recognize until we are ready to open our eyes to things impossible, unexpected, and often last minute…or more likely, <u>exactly</u> when we need them. This is being "held in love," and it comes in all forms, shapes, and sizes. It IS there in all of our lives, if only we open our eyes to see it.

---

(1) ACIM Workbook lesson 100: "My part is essential to God's plan for salvation"
  Lines: 2.1; 6.1; 8.1-8.3
(2) ACIM Workbook, lesson 99: "Salvation is my only function here" lines 5.4-5.5

*The idea of the "guardian" comes from Caroline Myss's interpretation of Toto in the Wizard of Oz., found in her book, *Sacred Contracts*. On page 172, she writes: *"Dorothy's guardian for the journey is Toto, the Latin word for 'everything'."*

**This chapter and the chapter, *A Perfect Day* were first published in the compilation *Held in Love*, edited by Molly Young Brown and Carolyn Wilbur Treadway

CHAPTER 4
Heartache

Shortly after I met JM, a year and several months after A., the "love of my life" walked out, I awoke in the night with a sharp pain in my chest. It was as if someone had ripped my heart out. The next day I awoke with a temperature, coughing, and body aches similar to those of the flu. I had trouble breathing and was diagnosed with tracheitis, which after several weeks unhealed, developed into bronchitis. This in turn did not completely heal; I coughed and coughed and my chest became more and more painful. I felt as if I could not breathe deeply, and though X-rays were taken and I was sent to consult a lung specialist, the doctors could not determine what was wrong.

I had always been in good health with strong lungs and heart, developed through regular swimming, walking, and yoga. Though I liked JM, this new young man who was attracted to me, and enjoyed his company, I could not forget A. and wondered if the pain in my chest were not psychosomatic. I often cried with grief at the thought of that relationship, and the burning in my chest would intensify. JM knew of my story with A. and believed my physical condition was related to the hurt I had experienced as a result of that unexpected break-up. Though I also believed in this connection, I could not release the pain; it was as if something needed to be *gotten off my chest.*

My work with subpersonalities in psychosynthesis had introduced me within myself to a sad, hurt, and very frightened little girl, also to a sophisticated 1950's-styled *femme fatale.* This latter character went into high gear to seduce, look good and be sexy shortly after I met JM. The more I worked with her to understand her needs, the more I realized she had also wanted to seduce and please A, to get him to <u>really</u> notice her and love her. I could see how this part of me sought the validation of a man, a romantic relationship to give me permission somehow to exist. It was frightening to recognize this, but the way I felt deep within. Though I could intellectually understand how this survival personality had developed, I could not change her views or beliefs.

Months later, after I was diagnosed with pericarditis (an inflammation of the membrane protecting the heart), forced to rest and remain quiet, avoiding any effort for two months, I felt as if my heart had a knife through it. The more I sat with this feeling and "focused" (1) the more I could see in my mind's eye the image of my *femme fatale* carrying a knife and wanting to kill someone, as if she wanted revenge. A part of me felt no matter how I wanted to move forward, turn the page, and get on with life, it was impossible to remove the knife from my heart – the bleeding would be unbearable, heart-breaking, too much. Consequently, no matter how it hurt, for the moment this symbolic knife had to stay.

I meditated on this feeling. Was the ripping out sensation I had experienced in early March designed to protect me from an even more horrific repressed childhood memory? Or was I finally experiencing all the pain, hurt and anger accumulated and repressed for so many years? Was I ready today to face the pain, betrayal, indifference, and neglect of my childhood? What was the message behind this symbolic knife, turning painfully in my heart? And now that the pain was recognized, would it go away?

> A journal excerpt May 28th:
> *I awake feeling tired and exhausted, and realize the doctor has said to rest. I don't "have to" get up: I'm supposed to rest. And, I'm in my own lovely bed in my little house in the woods, not in the hospital. Brownie came up to see if I was awake, then went downstairs again without disturbing me. All is well!*
>
> *I am to rest for a month, and I realize the injunction is for **me**, the loving thing to do for myself. I am no longer in my 20's or 30's or in the sad saga of my childhood, or in a broken marriage, or even in the throes of the heart-wrenching disappointment with A. It is today. I am 50. I have pericarditis. I need to rest in order to get better, and circumstances have cooperated to allow me to do just that. I have no work, people or distractions to take my attention off me.*
>
> *If it could speak, what does my heart want to tell me? "It's time, time to heal, time to share your truth, and let it go. Write it all out; write the book. This is the time. You have the setting, time, and space. It couldn't be more perfect."*

One month later in June I am much better. I write at the lake:
> *I swam freely, easily, and openly. The water is clear, cool, fresh, blue-green, and lovely. It is quiet and warm; a cooling*

breeze blows gently. In swimming, a perfect book title came to me: Unreasonable Love: Reclaiming Self (2) Reclaiming self is what I am doing in my therapy sessions with Mme F, reclaiming myself. In today's session I suddenly remembered how as a child I was afraid to go to the bathroom, afraid to "let go", to "make a mess", be dirty, leave a trace or a smell. I was afraid to leave signs of existence and do what is natural…no wonder I have a problem today letting go.

My story reminded me of Misty, a beautiful little dog I adopted in Paris when I was first married. This little dog had been abused and traumatized, used for animal experimentation and hit when she tried to eat. For months she could not tolerate human presence nearby when she needed to eat; she was so afraid that she cowered. It was painful to see for I could relate to this feeling of not being allowed to exist…always cringing. Tortured, used, abused. Recently, in speaking to a friend, I had mentioned Misty and the horror she had probably gone through (though she was unable to tell me). My friend said: "you brought her back to life with love." Other people had said the very same thing to me when Misty was alive. Some had even gone so far as to say that if they were to reincarnate, they wanted to come back as my dog, like Misty…

As I write I feel the deep love I felt for Misty, and remember when she died how much I felt I had lost love. Today, Brownie lays his head on my left arm and cuddles into my hip and leg. He is my "guardian," always watchful, present, protective, caring. When I tell him what a beautiful boy he is, I feel such warmth inside. I am in admiration of his unconscious ability to be himself, to just **be**. How peaceful, poised, and statuesque he becomes when I speak to him in that way! These days he barely leaves my side, as if he can sense how much I need love; he follows me around the house and plops down uncomplainingly the way Misty did many years ago.

* * *

In my therapy session, I unexpectedly blurted out: "*I couldn't say 'no'. I had to go along with it all; there was no way out*". Somehow, I knew what my father said was not true…all the stories I was to relate at school concerning who he was and what he did. Yet today, I am still tied to what my therapist called "the madness of my progenitors" ("*la folie de mes progeniteurs*"). On one hand I can see how I never bought into everything that my father said, but I couldn't say anything to anyone outside. There seemed to be no way out. As soon as I did tell someone with "authority" (my therapist), I started having recurring nightmares in which I had one split second to grab my little, emaciated Brownie boy, and RUN from a Gestapo-like concentration camp. I would awaken in terror, holding my breath for fear of being heard.

In real life I also ran...across an ocean...putting to use the only resources I had: my intellect and my facility for French. Music and singing had been taboo at home, but French was a "cultured", thus acceptable foreign language that I easily picked up by ear. My question today was why, as an adult, I viewed my efforts to get by in life with contempt? I had been running from madness, said my therapist. Without intellectually understanding this – the knowing that pushed me to flee was deeper – today I felt I had failed miserably in life. I was alone, with no family and no job.

On one level, though I had difficulty feeling it, I had succeeded. I could see the "brand" or injunction to say nothing and to feel insignificant was still present and operating. An ingrained, hidden voice seemed to instruct:

> *Don't cut the link with your family, or you'll go spiralling down into a pit of bottomless death... black and sickening, spinning so fast you want to throw up. You never land, so you're destined to constantly spin out of control, spiraling rapidly downwards, never getting your balance and never hitting ground.*

This was a foreboding, threatening voice I heard deep within me. I could see where my aversion to amusement park rides came from, as well as my carsickness. I could feel the fear of being hit, until you think you just can't take another breath. The breath is knocked out of you, and you fear you can't get another one. Despite my adult present reality, far from childhood control and domination, within me lived that fear of being beaten down, and a hidden belief to remain loyal, loyal to the madness, loyal to the family, loyal to what I had experienced.

This internal formatting continues the abuse spiral sometimes for generations, long after the initial situation is over if healing is not sought to take its place. But healing does not happen overnight, and it does not occur simply because we decide or decree it.

* * *

From my vantage point on the other side of the lake, safe from humanity, I watch people arrive and settle in. I see horseback riders and boys throwing stones in the lake from the pier. I see two fathers play with little girls in the water, and wonder what it is like to have a father touch you safely and play with you when you are small.

I see a couple swim gently; the man catches up to the woman and embraces her body for a moment. My body throbs as I watch, and I remember with longing what it feels like to be enfolded in the water, touched and hugged with gentleness and love. I plunge into the water again to escape this aching feeling, and swim effortlessly. I feel strong and safe, so safe in the water. Water has always been a quiet refuge for me.

When I get out, I sit and feel the ache, how I long to be touched by gentle, kind, human hands…how I long to be allowed to live, to be…the way the playful German shepherd I see on the other side of the lake, and the way Brownie, merely <u>is</u>, without fear.

---

(1) "Focusing"- a technique developed by Eugene Gendlin, professor at the University of Chicago. This inward focusing technique allows the body to communicate through images, color and other symbolism, sending a message behind a sensation or feeling. Eugene T. Gendlin, *Focusing, How to gain direct access to your body's knowledge*

(2) This complemented information I received the night I returned from the Findhorn Foundation in Scotland in October months previously. I had awoken with the message: *"your book is entitled "l'Amour Déraisonné."* The words came to me in French and mean "unreasonable love." It was about 4 a.m.; tired, I wrote them down in my journal and went back to sleep, the critic part of me saying: *"a book? What book?* ***You*** *can't write a book…"*

CHAPTER 5

Losing Power

Early one morning in the summer, a violent thunderstorm knocked out my broadband Internet box. The company providing the box and the broadband service was called *Alice*, and the box totally burned out by the storm, I was cut-off from the world wide web. I needed to sort out the logistics of declaration and exchange, or I would continue to be without email and Internet connection, further isolating me in my day-to-day living.

Now that I had explored personal healing, I no longer viewed this event as castigation from heaven or punishment for personal worthlessness, but nonetheless I knew the sooner I got on the phone with the commercial, technical and other *Alice* personnel, the sooner I would receive a new broadband box, which meant the sooner I would be up and running in the world of the world wide web. A good little scout and eager beaver, I buckled down to deal with "musak" and long phone holds, before getting the *Alice* technical red tape accomplished and a new box ordered. Now I could relax and get on with the rest of life, knowing that today I would not be dealing with emails and Internet work. In some ways this was an opportunity from the universe to go inward, work on my book, and continue exercises in my psychosynthesis training.

The following morning a text message arrived saying my *Alice* box had arrived at my village post office. *YIPPEE!* I almost bounded into the car. Fortunately I decided to call first, and lo and behold, there was no trace of the package at the post office. I tried to follow up, then decided to let the universe follow its own timing, i.e. sit back and wait for the postman, who undoubtedly had the package in his van.

I waited, viewing this delay as another opportunity to let go and allow. Still, I did not dare leave the house for an instant in case the replacement mailman (this is the month of August and all of France is on vacation) arrived, only to leave without delivering my precious box. At about 5 p.m. I saw the yellow postal van careen down my country lane and speed past my house as if demons from hell were in pursuit. I was left with the settling dust and the returned quiet of the late summer afternoon, but no box.

* * *

Saturday arrived and I was sure my box would arrive. It must, since I was leaving for a week early Monday morning and the postal service did not deliver Sundays or Saturday afternoons. If I was not present to sign for what was fast becoming an aggravating box, the package would be returned to the company and I would need to start the entire process all over again! I could feel the tension rising in me. Wishing to be proactive, I called the post office again to verify the whereabouts of my package. To my surprise nothing could be confirmed. They still had no trace of the package. Could I give them the registered number?

Alice had not given me a number. So, before breakfast, back to the phone I went…to more *"musak",* holds, repetitive company jingles…until I could feel my morning peace totally obscured. I finally got a live person, who informed me they needed to give me the commercial department. I went back to holding…more jingles, my patience wearing thin. Within myself I kept giving myself a pep talk: *"hang in there – we're almost there."*

Finally, the person on the line said, *"we can't access your file."*

"Why not?" I asked. They couldn't explain. I should call back later that afternoon. I explained that the post office would be closed by then. They repeated they couldn't help me, and then repeated this *ad infinitum* until it sounded like a robotic voice. And that was the end of the conversation. I was cut off, with the only explanation being, *"can't help you."*

My sense of peace and power were now gone, evaporated, out the window! I was furious and frustrated. I again tried calling the post office. After much waiting, I was informed the postman had not yet left, so the package was still potentially at the post office.

GREAT! *"Could I talk with the post man?"* I asked politely.

"Oh no…" was the response.

"Was there a way to contact him?" I asked.

Apparently the atmosphere at the post office was tense with this replacement postman. There came a long pause… then the suggestion: *"try this number and see if they answer."*

YES!

Fortunately, someone did answer and I was able to explain my problem, then go to the post office and find the infamous package. It was lying on the sidewalk in the sun with a few other packages like a pile of trash! To make a long story short, I got the box and was able to reconfigure the connection and set myself up in the world of virtual reality. But the reason I am telling you this story is not to bore you, nor to solicit your pity for inefficient postal workers in France, or for poor neglected *Alice* clients, such as myself. I am writing this is to demonstrate how easily I lost my power and sense of balance over an outside event for which I had no control.

We live mistakenly with the belief we can, and <u>should</u> control everything in our immediate sphere of influence, or life; yet, lo and behold, we cannot. When this lack of power was blatantly thrown in my face concerning the delivery of my infamous *Alice* box, instead of reciting the *Serenity Prayer*, and accepting it with grace and ease, I went ballistic!

> *A Course in Miracles,* Workbook lesson 69 says:
> *"My grievances hide the light of the world in me."*

We are reminded in this lesson that we are trying *"to reach the light in you… trying to see past the veil of darkness… We are trying to let the veil be lifted, and to see the tears of God's Son disappear in the sunlight."* (ACIM Workbook lesson 69 lines 2.1-5)

My tears did not disappear in the sunlight, perhaps because I insisted things go the way I wanted them to go. I was filled with grievances during this little event. From <u>my</u> perspective, everyone involved (starting with *Alice* and finishing with the post office) were incompetent. From my perspective, **"I had work to do, and, why did this have to happen and disturb my peace and ability to get on with life? REALLY!"** This sounded like my Queen speaking…

I could see how I lost my grip; no one made me crazy or upset. I did it. I was always in control, but I gave my power away to an Internet box! This event reminded me of a story world-renowned lecturer and author, Caroline Myss, shares in one of her workshops and on a C.D. She recounts her own experience of going crazy over a taxi driver in Chicago, who threw a MacDonald's hamburger wrapper out of his car onto Michigan Avenue. She went ballistic too. In retelling the story she advises: *"if you're going to lose your cool, and your power, make sure it's over something worthwhile."* (1)…a MacDonald's hamburger paper…an Internet box?

Losing my sense of peace and personal power did not contribute to anything, other than high blood pressure. I don't think it helped me to receive the box. What is certain is that after this event, I needed to lie in my hammock, breathe deeply, and let the incident go, as if it had had a traumatizing effect on my life. Seriously, was it worth it? I saw how far I had to go to become the person I wanted, and live life peacefully, despite events and happenings.

(1) Story told by Caroline Myss on her recorded workshop: "The Call to Live a Symbolic Life"

CHAPTER 6

Love and *All that Jazz*

The myth of « falling in love »

« *Je ne t'aime pas – voilà…* » *(I don't love you – that's all.)*
These words came from JM, my new boyfriend.
"Gee whiz…here we go again…"

We had been getting on fine, truly enjoying each other's company, it seemed. We loved similar music, dancing, walking in nature…and adored animals. We talked and talked, exploring our pasts, fears, limits…talking and sharing for hours. I found him gentle, understanding, "wise beyond his years." To be truthful, sometimes I found it hard to bear his constant talking! Though often interesting, there were times when I needed silence. Who really knew the answer to a number of the questions we evoked, and did it matter?

Now the question was moot; he wasn't *in love* with me. From one day to the next we were no longer "a number", or "together". He went from sending me three messages a day with his sweet sign-off: *"your JM"*…*"I tenderly kiss you all over"*… calling me every day and addressing me with French terms of endearment such as *"ma puce," "Minou,"* to… nothing, silence.

"That's all, folks!"

Though I was not *in love* with him, the sudden change of heart/mind left a painful, empty void. This was my first try at a relationship with a man since my painful break-up/betrayal with A. Though I had been vigilant (not wanting to go too fast), there were a number of things I enjoyed about JM, and I had been on the verge of feeling I could be happy with someone else… *Bang!* My barely healed heart broke open again.

* * *

"*I am not in love*". What do these words mean anyway? A friend of mine had recently said something that rang true: "*Being in love is for yourself. Loving is for the other person.*"

This statement seemed to corroborate what JM subsequently conveyed to me in an email:

I was only in love <u>once</u> (with my ex-wife); no question about it, she made me suffer, and I am no longer in love with her today, but I need that feeling of wanting to give all; it gives me wings, and I need to feel that again... Sorry.

Within me, my "femme fatale" became <u>livid</u> and threw out interjections of "*jerk, asshole!*" She ranted up and down:

What? You're not in love? Ha! That's not what came across in your messages, and that puppy-dog look of admiration you beamed on me each time we were together. What about all the admiring things you said about me to everybody you knew? You neglected your friends to be with me. Your best friend called me 'Casper' (the friendly ghost), since all he heard from you, was: 'Olivia, Olivia...'.

Naturally JM was not in love with me. He couldn't be in love with someone like me, because he was caught in another myth or ego game. <u>He</u> needed a woman he could "save". His knight archetype/ subpersonality (1) desperately needed its ego stroked by a partner who was in dire need of help, someone he could rescue. This dynamic had attracted him to in his ex-wife, a woman who was depressed, unable to work, and in anxious need of a knight. So JM had symbolically jumped on his stallion, ridden to the rescue, and fallen blindly *in love*.

The partnership served both parties for a time, as Dr. Delis explains in his book, *The Passion Paradox* (2). The relationship worked until the disdain of dependence erased looks of gratitude and love, replacing them with disgust, distaste and contempt. At that point, no matter how hard JM tried to please, he failed, and elicited tirades of anger, upset and aversion.

One day he had enough. Unconsciously, JM's "victim" went so far to re-establish his wife's attention that he accepted a physical task at work, he unconsciously knew he should not; it ruined his back. Today, he can prove his 45% handicap with an official card from the State health services. His efforts had been an unconscious attempt to make her care for him… The tactic did not work. When he showed he was in real physical pain and in need of nurturing himself, she flashed him a look of utter aversion and he knew it was over. His marriage was over, and he crawled away in pain and abject hurt.

What did this have to do with me? After our brief relationship I could see my own pattern. A part of me, the "poor, forlorn waif," had been attracted to his "knight", like JM's ex-wife had been drawn to him. But my waif was growing up, not needy enough to satisfy his knight. Naturally he could not sprout the necessary wings he needed to soar, and fall madly and irrevocably (is it ever *irrevocably*?) in love. After some exploration I could see a similar pattern, need and unconscious motives that had attracted me to A. My sad, fearful little waif had always sought a knight in shining armor to save her. Even with my ex-husband, we used to laugh in graduate school when he arrived in his old, gray Chevrolet in the cold, snowy Boston winter. He would announce: *"the knight in shining Chevrolet has arrived!"*

* * *

Reflections from survival personalities:

As part of my psychosynthesis exploration and in an exercise to become better acquainted with my subpersonalities, I wrote in late May 2008:

Last week three or four days before JM changed heart, I was getting acquainted with my "femme fatale." I could see her wearing a gauzy peignoir in a comfortable bedroom (4 poster-bed), feeling despair and upset. Deep down she felt soiled and tainted; she could never have what other women have: a loving husband and family, someone who cares.

She had been tainted, 'raped', marked; … no "good" man would want her. She lay prostrate on the bed in tears. (It reminded me of how I had once felt about a guy in college, someone I thought of as good, upright and moral. I felt he never would want someone like me if he knew about the black muck inside of me. Though attracted, I didn't ever try to seduce him – we remained friends and I looked at him from afar.

I could see how this survival personality had developed. For the *femme fatale*, the only way to get a guy is to seduce – physically and intellectually, quietly, surreptitiously. I could seduce or attract with my intellect and with my exotic foreign background. My *femme fatale* had sought to seduce A. and had fallen for him. Perhaps she hoped against hope that the curse or incurable brand would be lifted, since she loved him. In my ego's script A. was to redeem the soiled past, but he didn't, and of course, he couldn't.

Today, using psychosynthesis, I wanted my *femme fatale* to know she was OK; the war was over. She need not rip my heart out to protect herself or take revenge. I wanted to care for her; I could feel her suffering and pain. "Special relationships" as the Course calls them, are doomed to failure. Because the ego's tactics cannot work, and our small sense of self is not all we are, this subpersonality's plan and tactics would always backfire, and the "nice" guy would always walk out, saying he was not "in love".

---

(1) For a fuller explanation of archetypes and subpersonalities, see:
Caroline Myss, *Sacred Contracts*, Molly Young Brown, *Growing Whole*, Firman and Gila, *Psychosynthesis A Psychology of the Spirit*, Piero Ferrucci, *What we May Be*.
(2) Dean Delis and Cassandra Phillips *The Passion Paradox*

What we live by, or self interest

Piero Ferrucci writes in his book, *What We May Be,* that *"Love is what we live by."*(1) **Do** we effectively live by love? Can we honestly say love is what guides our relationships and the way we treat our planet?

As I read the words, *"love is what we live by,"* in my mind's eye I see the cutting down of the rainforest in the Amazon and the widespread destruction of the planet. I feel Mother Earth or "Gaia", crying, hurting, and bleeding. An image I recently saw on the news appears to me of two portly, self-satisfied Minnesota farmers, excited about the lucrative offers they were receiving on their farm to plant corn… not for food, for ethanol!

Against a backdrop of world food riots and people starving due to skyrocketing food prices, in the West we still want to run hungry, gas-guzzling SUV's. And if corn will do it, so be it! Yet, love is what we live by…

David Lovelock (a renowned British scientist) in his book, *The Revenge of Gaia* (2) explains how signs of global warming and imminent danger to the planet have been visible for years. Have we paid attention? Lovelock portends the planet is a live entity, and as it heats up, the icecaps melt, catastrophic weather patterns abound, and *Gaia* screams out in pain, and anger. Heedless, we continue to burn down natural habitats where plants and animals have thrived for centuries. These simple living entities, fragile and beautiful, have helped us maintain health, longevity, and well being. Yet, we are too short-sighted to see we are annihilating and destroying our own future. Is this short-term pleasure principle the extent to which our consciousness has developed? Unconscious and immature, we seem unable to heed the signs of demise and the writing on the wall.

As I write, it thunders and rumbles and roars around me. I am reminded of a high school play years ago where to create thunder, we used large panels of aluminium that were ruffled and buffeted to create a threatening, rumbling sound. It's raining heavily, again… Everyday, for weeks, we have had gray skies, storms, and unprecedented amounts of rain. It's mid June. I live in the south of France; the weather at this time of year is usually clement. For the first time in over ten years, the water has come down so fast and hard, it is almost leaking into the house.

I live on a hill above the village, so flooding has never been a concern. Still it rains, and pours. I go outside to bail the water away from my side door; for the first time it seems high enough to enter the sunroom! The rumbling amazes me, clanging and menacing in a back and forth exchange of sound through the trees off to the west. It sounds like an irate, angry argument among the gods. Who will throw down the thunderbolt of retribution onto the unconscious human beings below, who are debasing and destroying the once beautiful, and now mutilated, raped and tortured daughter, Gaia?

The earth is weeping; every day she pours out her pain in torrential rains, and rumbles her anger… and despair. Yesterday, as I sat in a similar storm (protected by an overhang on the porch), listening to the grumbling thunder, the rumbling seemed to reverberate in the depths of my chest. It seemed to say we couldn't have warmth, sunshine and peace – we couldn't allow ourselves, since we are all guilty and undeserving, or believe ourselves to be. What have we done to our protective, nourishing Mother Earth? How have we repaid her for her beauty, life-giving nourishment, and abundance? Look at the storms, floods, heat waves and earthquakes. Are we blind? How long will it take for us to awaken and to question? Everywhere on earth people seek to increase personal advantage. Consequently, we take, use and consume, with little thought for tomorrow, not even for our own species, let alone for other creatures that share the planet with us. They have rights, "*or do they?*" we answer unconsciously, as if we, in some way have the right to decide.

In the "developed" world we blindly use the planet's natural resources faster than they can be replenished. We don't seriously explore sustainable solutions; we would have to change our behavior patterns, e.g. walk a little, think of others, respect other cultures' and countries' beliefs in interdependence, harmony with nature, and other less individualistic values. Each person focuses on his/her (or his/her group's) own selfish wants and desires…it's all about instant gratification. What can I buy or obtain <u>now</u>, in order to distract me from a gnawing pain and void I feel within, a lack of love. To cover my pain, I will lie, distort information, manipulate, connive, use, consume, and even kill those who I believe are outside of my in-group, country or tribe… **Is that love?**

If we look at relationships within our families, what can we say about love there? Even in personal relationships, we can't accept the love given to us, in the form it comes. We have needs…so many needs, and we believe it is the other person's role to satisfy those needs. Alas, it's never quite right; the person is too *critical, not understanding, distant*…there is always some judgment made to show something is lacking.

The Course speaks of *"the scarcity principle"* as a belief that runs the world. The more I look around, listen, and observe, the more I see this limiting belief at work. I am not advocating maintaining relationships with partners, friends, or lovers, who criticize, or in other ways disrespect you. But isn't it interesting how in our modern world, love often seems to go awry? Over and over, relationships last awhile, then break up in angry retribution and arguments in court. Or, protagonists remain together (for financial or other fear-related reasons), living in cold, distant avoidance, or critical judgment and projection of unhappiness.

* * *

My ex-boyfriend, JM, had left less than a month ago. No matter how much esteem he felt for me, or how much we enjoyed each other's company, or because of mutual interests, he simply was not "in love."

Now the excuses were expressed: I didn't appreciate police movies or heavy metal rock music. He felt the problem was **he** was too eclectic – he loved jazz (both funk and big-band) and like me, enjoyed tango. For a while there had been the illusion of complicity or togetherness. What were the real reasons, I wondered? In Western culture, media, storybooks, family beliefs and teachings feed us an illusory and unattainable vision of love. Yet, *A Course in Miracles,* workbook lesson 127 clearly states:

"There is no love but God's."

The lesson begins by expressing my own beliefs concerning love:
Perhaps you think that different kinds of love are possible. Perhaps you think there is a kind of love for this, a kind of love for that; a way of loving one, another way of loving still another.
(ACIM lesson 127 Lines 1.1-1.2)

Truthfully, I did believe this, and look where it had gotten me… The lesson continues:

> *Love is one. It has no separate parts and no degrees; no kinds nor levels, no divergencies and no distinctions. It is like itself, unchanged throughout. It never alters with a person or a circumstance. It is the Heart of God, and also of His Son.*
> (Lines 1.3-1.7)

This love I had never experienced, but as I read on I was reminded why…

> *No law the world obeys can help you grasp love's meaning. What the world believes was made to hide love's meaning, and to keep it dark and secret. There is not one principle the world upholds but violates the truth of what love is, and what you are as well.*
>
> *Seek not within the world to find your Self. Love is not found in darkness and in death.*
> (ACIM Lesson 127 lines 5.1-6.2)

This would explain why love is seemingly so elusive; we are looking in the wrong place, and the qualities we have projected onto love are false. As I mused, I remembered, the Course's introduction:

> *The course does not aim at teaching the meaning of love, for that is beyond what can be taught. It does aim, however, at removing the blocks to the awareness of love's presence, which is your natural inheritance.* (ACIM intro. Lines 1.6-7)

---

(1) A chapter title in Piero Ferrucci's book, *What we may be*
(2) David Loveluck, *The Revenge of Gaia*

Part II

CHAPTER 7

Healing
Healing through Tango

I had not danced tango for a year. For four years A. had been my regular partner and the painful association was too present, so I had abandoned the association, gone inward for healing, and left tango far out in left field. To all intents and purposes I had not danced for a year. To be precise, I <u>had</u> gone to Paris to tango two nights in March. Though not a dancer himself, JM had asked to accompany me, so I had been escorted. This felt comfortable and safe, though it was still up to me to find potential partners.

The Paris festival was rich and sensual, with a magnificent orchestra, deep colors of blacks and reds, flowing fabrics and fluid bodies. As the evening progressed on Saturday, I must confess to a remarkable experience! I met a divine dancer from Geneva. This unexpected experience reconciled me with life, dance, and a knowing that dance **is** a life-giving force for me: I LOVE IT!

As a result of my Parisian good fortune, when July approached and with it an important Argentinean tango festival in a nearby village, I took courage in hand and signed onto the association's web list in search of a dance partner. A man from Paris contacted me. We signed up for a class, and I was reassured I would be accompanied, so I felt an unspoken "permission" to be present. Thirty-six hours before the beginning of the festival, one day before I was to meet my new dance partner, I received a phone call saying he had hit a wild boar on his motorbike, returning from a Parisian "*milonga*"! He had broken his hip, was in the hospital, and was in no condition to dance!

Despite my strengthening and healing work to release past conditioning, the habitual inner recording clicked on, and I couldn't help wondering… "WHY? Why me? And what is all this about?"

Instead of believing something better was on its way, deep inside the feelings of panic resurfaced in floodgates:

"*Oh no, I'm again totally on my own! I know no one; no one will dance with me. I'll have a horrible class partner who'll step on my toes and can't lead his way out of a paper bag.*"

I tried to reassure myself that there was no reason to imagine the worst... I didn't even know the partner I was signed up with. I had never seen him, let alone danced with him...it was all unknown anyway. Despite my internal pep talk, it took all my strength and courage to go to the first evening dance, alone. And, during this evening, **who** do you think came up behind me, and touched me on both shoulders?

A! He was not alone, but accompanied by the little Japanese girlfriend I had felt my knees buckle over a few months ago, when he had nonchalantly informed me that *of course* they not only danced, but slept together, since **we** were no longer together...

This evening I was totally taken aback. He asked me to dance. I accepted. I was not dancing, and did not feel any ill feelings at that moment. We danced with great mediocrity. I must admit he was never a great dancer. He could maneuver a number of fancy figures, but not necessarily in time with the music...vaguely, but not exactly in time. I had often felt that dancing with him when he was offbeat, was as pleasant as having someone run his fingernails across a blackboard.

After the two or three tangos of tango etiquette, I thanked him and sat down. I felt no anger, no upset, nothing. I knew I was over him, finally. The year had been long and painful, with much soul-searching, crying, deep hurt, and sense of betrayal, but that was over. I saw A. today as a man who was not in tune with feeling. How could he dance tango, other than in form and appearance? You need to be able to listen to what is subtle, unspoken, that which seethes and surges within your being, in harmony with the music, and in communication with the person in your arms.

My week at the festival pushed me to turn continually within, to find the perseverance and strength to go out each evening, <u>alone</u>. But, I went. I made myself visible. *"I was seen"*... thus going against a family conditioning or injunction. Initially nothing unusual happened, but I lay the ground works for something. I was present, and I asked to dance.

I met two new partners; one was relatively inexperienced, but the other danced beautifully. In a game entitled, "The American Quarter Hour", women were supposed to choose their partner, and I almost did not pick D., since he was thin, gangly and reminded me a bit of the scarecrow in MGM's film, *The Wizard of OZ*. Appearances can be deceiving, and if I recall correctly, in the MGM film with Judy Garland, Ray Bolger, an outstanding dancer, played the part of the scarecrow...

D. was also an outstanding dancer! He had been dancing for 10 years, was relaxed, assured, gentle, and created a secure environment in which to follow; all in all, dancing with him was a total pleasure. I had only dreamed of meeting a partner like this. Our very first dance, we bypassed tango etiquette and danced several dances one after the other, finally saying *"thank you"*, and *"à une prochaine fois"(until the next time)*. This was my first step into paradise that week.

D. and I crossed paths again, danced, then danced again. By the middle of the week, he would come to find me, and by Thursday, we must have danced and danced, and danced, the way regular partners did… We were obviously noticed, since the photographer said to us later: *"how's it going, lovers?"* In D.'s arms, I existed and was seen; I felt comforted, cared for, and floated on air… I felt I could dance forever, eyes closed, oblivious to the crowd of dancers around us, unafraid of stumbling, kicking anyone, or making a *faux pas*.

D. twirled me, cuddled me, comforted me… We laughed or smiled at misunderstood signals or last minute improvisations, due to the obstacle of other couples in our path. I never felt tired with him. He never weighed on me or became disgruntled if I misunderstood a signal; in no way was disharmony created. We spun and glided effortlessly through the crowded couples, his steady guiding taking advantage of a sudden opening, and moving us together as if we were one body and mind. It was <u>total bliss</u>. My tango week was a great success, and because I stepped out, alone, I felt stronger, more solid and real somehow.

Loving Kindness

Today I will not judge or hurt myself with thoughts or criticisms. I will now treat myself only with loving-kindness.
Legacy of the Heart, Wayne Muller

No matter how natural it may seem to receive love from another person (partner, parents, family, or friends), ultimately the only one who can give you love is yourself. Western society indoctrinates us otherwise and we spend most of our lives seeking outside ourselves for validation, care, and love. For me, when it became clear that my family was incapable, the men in my life too lost, scared, or immature, friends too preoccupied with their challenges, problems, and pain... and time ticking on... that I began to accept this fact. I was alone, or so it felt.

What I *knew* was a past that hurt, had been destructive and uncaring, leaving scars, lots of scars. The work I had been doing in therapy showed me the extent to which I hurt, and how deep inside I was still afraid. This is what I felt. No matter how I kept trying to reason with myself with messages of: "*it's time to get over it*", "*move on, be an adult, grow up*"...a part of me hurt, and was terrified.

The way to heal is to stop the war against yourself, stop inflicting pain, and stop the internal diatribe: "*you're not good enough*" or "*look at...*" (almost anyone in my entourage sufficed to show how lacking I was). Deeper than the conscious thoughts, were the ingrained feelings of unworthiness and fear that I had no right to exist. Faced with these feelings, I felt more horrified than compassionate and loving. My scared little chipmunk subpersonality (like my scared little girl) elicited more pity from me than a desire to care. Was I incapable of caring? Both Brownie and Misty had been beings I had cared for, loved, and patiently nursed back to life... I **was** capable of kindness and gentleness. Why not use it for myself?

A recent session with my therapist revealed a symbolic split in my physical body. The right side seemed to reflect the capable, accomplished teacher and trainer, while the left communicated the need for quiet, nature, green and gentleness. This part of me was fearful of close human interaction, fearful of erratic and potentially violent changes of behavior. My left side appeared to my mind's eye in a meditation as "*stubble, no growth, dry*". The tiny chipmunk I saw in the meditation wanted to hide in the brown leaves of the forest floor, so no one would see him.

Nonetheless, this side of myself, when asked what it needed, seemed to respond: "*to be seen.*" It needed kindness, gentleness and love to grow and flourish. I was starving for this attention from another person, but my therapist insisted it had to come from me. Intuitively, though I wasn't sure how to respond, I knew it was too risky to trust anyone else with this important and delicate task. Gentleness, kindness, and love had to come from me – there were no two ways about it. The question was: *how?*

CHAPTER 8

A Perfect Day*

Already late August, I could feel the kiss of fall in the air. Today was Sunday and I was alone with no plans. I had been again struggling with solitude and feelings of heavy, oppressive loneliness. I decided to take advantage of this final Sunday morning when the grocery store would be open, to go out; at the end of the summer vacation, in "*la France profonde*," once the tourists left, Sundays would return to their sacred quietness... the one day a week no one worked except mornings in bakeries and food markets. (Food **is** sacred in France, and consequently, exceptions can be made in work legislation).

The day was crisp and partially sunny, but promising to be dry, with the incisive edge of clarity fall brings. I knew it would be good to swim, though I wondered what the water would be like at the lake. It had been getting cooler and quite chilly at night; today only registered about 25° C. I arrived at the lake where only a young couple with a very cute, and happy little dog played on the makeshift beach. I watched the little dog repeatedly (yet with great joy) jump into the water in search of a little stick its masters mechanically threw. While they seemed rather blasé and rigid in their actions, the little dog was totally in the moment, joyous, barking, aware only of his stick, the water, and the joy he had from retrieving that stick for his beloved masters. I realized for a moment that life is made only of moments. Each moment comes and goes, bringing us much to see and enjoy, if only we can be present, really present... instead of preoccupied with worries or plans for the future, and regrets or analysis of the past.

I settled myself at a new spot, a place where I had never sat, despite my many years frequenting this lake. The grass was like a mown lawn and led easily down to the water. It was very sunny and quiet, except for the sounds of happy barking to my left. Brownie went to the water's edge to have a drink, wet his feet, and then proceeded to demonstrate <u>his</u> joy, running crazily around me in circles, rolling over repeatedly like a circus dog, and throwing his own stick in the air. Decidedly, there was joy and happiness in the air!

I lay in the sun; it was warm, and quiet. The place and weather were absolutely beautiful. Still I was unable to totally enjoy that beauty – I was lonely and tired of being alone all the time. I lived alone and was looking for work; though I loved my quiet little house in the woods, I was isolated. I felt I needed to leave to find companionship. For several months I had stopped fighting to "get out there" and be with people (anyone to avoid the loneliness), consequently I found myself more and more alone. To be honest, I was proud of how well I was doing. The quiet and regular aloneness was not as bad as I had anticipated, and on the whole I enjoyed the quiet and felt it was my only door to communion with my true Self, or with the Divine. But lately I felt impatient, like I had done my "cloistering"; it was time to get out, serve, do something, work…and meet people! Why did no one call or contact me? Why did I live in such isolation? My heart ached from feeling abandoned and my chest felt heavy and oppressed, a memory of recent pericarditis.

I went in for a swim. No one was around. The young couple had left and it was still early for the average Frenchman to be out, given the long, traditional Sunday lunch. Brownie sat with my clothes and towel, and I swam, back and forth in the middle of the lake. The water, though cool at first, felt fresh, clean, and lovely. My body moved effortlessly, with strength; my breathing was easy… Up and down I swam in the middle of the lake. I felt no fear, only the easiness of my movements, and the sure support of the water. I wondered briefly… if anyone could see me, would they liken me to a dolphin or other water creature playing in its element? I realized how lucky I was to be so at ease in water. I am, thanks to all those swimming lessons my grandmother forced down my throat years ago in Chicago when I was eight years old. Water is my element…cleansing, calming, and caring for me. I have never felt afraid in water; I adore it, and am drawn to it like a moth to light.

When I had my fill, I swam back to Brownie and got out to dry in the sun. I no longer felt lonesome, just refreshed, cleansed, anchored. As I sat on my mat, the warm sun beating down on me, I watched the water move. Sometimes the wind would gently whip up the surface and push the water into fast moving wave ripples; at other times it seemed to twinkle in the sun while moving happily in the direction of the current. I was aware it did not say *"no"*, or in any way resist or counter the flow of what came. I noticed the tall grasses growing at the edge of the water where I sat; they also moved with the wind when it blew. I looked up at the blue sky with big, billowy clouds that passed now in front of the sun. The sky did not seem to shout angrily at the clouds to get out of the way: "*you're covering up my blueness!*" I remembered how things change, how big, angry storms brew and the sky turns gray and fills with dark, menacing clouds.

Nature does not resist, question, or fight. It just <u>is</u>, and <u>does</u>. Storms come and go; the wind blows, then dies down… grasses lie flat, and then stand tall again in the sun. The surface of the lake is pushed by the wind, and then becomes calm, quiet, and pancake-like. Why was **I** resisting *what is*? Why not go with the flow? People come and go – they always have in my life. There is no reason to think I will always be alone, and if I am to be so today, resisting or pushing to manoeuvre company will not bring me serenity. Equanimity and serenity were qualities I wanted to cultivate; nature responds with equanimity – why not me? Whether I like it or not, as Thich Nhat Hanh teaches, and Molly Young Brown clearly stated in her book, *Growing Whole*:

> *I am of the nature to grow old; I am of the nature to become ill, I am of the nature to die, and everything in my life that is dear to me, (or not so) are of the nature to change.* (1)

Life is impermanent. How many times had I heard that in Buddhist retreats or teachings? Today, in my life I was in transition, change, and flux. Why resist, or find it unusual? Life is change – this is one thing we can count on…and that death will come to the body we inhabit. Nothing else is certain; yet we continually live as if nothing will or should, change in our lives. We resist a change in situation (new job or lose of one), lose of a life partner (divorce, death, or mere change of mind), change of abode (or the need to).

Today I was alone and I fought it as if it were a flaw in the script. I had accepted solitude for a few months while I was healing from my past pain, but the longer time weighed; I didn't like it. A part of me said: "*I am ready to have someone in my life…enough already…*" Yet, no matter how much I anguished, complained, felt sad or out of sync, I was in no way able to change "*what is*".

Life is a series of moments; they come and go like clouds in the sky, like our breath. We can be aware of them and live them as they come…or we cannot. But come they will, nonetheless. My sister had said on the phone, just the day before, "*We think we are in the driver's seat, but we aren't really.*" This perfect day I had been given another lesson in faith and support; why did I fight so? In many ways, God is like the water that supports me every time I go swimming. I don't question each time: *"is **this** water/pool/sea/lake going to support me?"* I <u>know it</u>, so in I plunge without fear or anxiety. What would happen if I approached every situation with that faith and knowing, as if every day were indeed a perfect day?

(1) These come from the Buddhist "Five Remembrances", translated by Thich Nhat Hanh in the "Plum Village Chanting Book" and recalled before meals on Sundays and other days at Plum Village, a retreat center in SW France.
Cited in Molly Young Brown, *Growing Whole,* 1993

*A Perfect Day was first published in the compilation *Held in Love.*

CHAPTER 9

Day to Day Healing

I awake to my alarm's incessant ringing. Ugh… the strident sound drags me from a deep, pleasant place of heavy repose and I cannot, just cannot let it go. I get up and turn the insistent thing off, then return to my warm bed with Brownie cuddled heavily on the quilt. "*Quilt*"… almost written like "*guilt*"…one quick turn of the pen changes everything.

I feel a twinge of guilt since it is already 9 o'clock and most people are already at work… not getting up, <u>at work</u>. Up they force themselves in the dark early morning, revolted against themselves or their true selves. In front of make-up or shaving mirrors they don masks for the day, disguising themselves in suits, stockings, dresses, tight sweaters, high-heeled shoes, or perhaps nail-studded boots and jeans. How far we live from ourselves… How far removed from our own home. I allow myself to sink into nothingness, still clinging to my mind's explanation: *"I just can't do it anymore; I'm so tired. Don't you see how trampled and destroyed, stepped on I was as a child…how "meurtrie"* as my psychologist says in French?

A part of me speaks: *"Can't you see I am finally trying to come into myself? If I don't take the time to discover myself at age 51, when will I find the time? When will I meet myself in this lifetime? When?"* The call of our roles and our conditioning is overpowering, incessant and seemingly reassuring and comforting… children, career, spouse or partner, their expectations… all is so pressing. Where does one find oneself in all the turmoil, in all the busyness?

I awake 45 minutes later, rested, at peace. My near-sighted eyes perceive brown leaves flying across my window as if they were flocks of birds. My mind must tell me they are leaves falling from the autumn trees, despite the resemblance to flocks of birds. I wonder…where are the birds? Where do they go to hide and be warm in the wet, cold drear of impending winter? Where are the birds? I think of the delicate, tiny red-breasted robin I saw a few days ago during a break in my weekend workshop for women.

Where are the birds <u>today</u> when it is so cold? Does anyone think of them? Does anyone remember them? Or are we too busy fighting with time in traffic jams, crowded subways and undergrounds, or wrestling with trains and crowds in order to arrive in neon lit offices where more "important" concerns take priority.

I arise and go downstairs in my richly quiet, little house in the woods. I am dying to write. I <u>need</u> to write, but first I must tend to the fire, or I will be cold like the little birds. My faithful 18-year-old wood-burning stove is carefully watching over the hot coals of the night before. I need only remove a shovel of fine ash (so fine it is like sand) and put in fresh, dry wood. As I feed my little stove, I feel how loyal, yet demanding it is. How hungry it is in winter and how sulky and cold it quickly becomes if I forget it. Today, like each morning, it is not forgotten, and I am soon comfortably ensconced on my couch with paper, pen, and…Brownie on my curled up legs, all of us enveloped and cosy in the deep silence and warmth, like a cosy, comforting quilt.

* * *

God, being Love, is also happiness. (ACIM, workbook lesson 103)
At some point things started to shift inside, ever so gently, but I could feel a shift nonetheless. I felt less scared, less angry, less incapable, and more peaceful; little bubblings of joy and happiness would gurgle up inside of me out of nowhere, over nothing, with no reason. I felt more distance from events and could see other people's foibles and their own fears of inadequacy, carefully covered and wrapped in glittery appearances, so no one would perceive them. *A Course in Miracles* explains: *"joy becomes what you expect to take the place of pain."* (ACIM Lesson 103 line 3.2)

What a beautiful idea! Instead of hurting and feeling bad, I could encounter a situation, professional or personal, and expect <u>joy</u>. I remembered new age slogans boasting, *"You get what you expect".* I had spent my life cringing and protecting myself, because I unconsciously expected things to be bad; they had repeatedly and unreasonably been so as a child, why would things change? I heard the same fear in my coaching sessions with the few clients I had recently attracted, as well as in my personal development seminars. We all seemed afraid of change, and in some 'sick' way, preferred to stay in our pain, wallow in self-pity, and resist healing or changing. I had read about this masochistic tendency and encountered it numerous times at untold seminars. I could see my own tendency to wallow and was unable to stop it – it seemed ingrained and burned deep within, like a CD you cannot overwrite. Still, somehow, something began to shift. How could I explain it? The change was subtle and quiet, but present.

In the Course there is a section in chapter 27, *The Healing of the Dream*, entitled *The Fear of Healing*. The opening asks:
> *Is healing frightening? To many, yes. For accusation is a bar to love, and damaged bodies are accusers.*
> (ACIM, Text, Chapter 27. II, Lines 1-3).

Two lines later the section describes a widely held and firmly ingrained belief:
> *Who has been injured by his brother, and could love and trust him still? He has attacked and will attack again. Protect him not, because your damaged body shows that **you** must be protected from him.* (Chapter 27.II lines 5-7)

As Ken Wapnick, specialist on The Course, repeats in his seminars: *"Who would I be without my dysfunctional family?"* I could <u>certainly</u> relate to that thought! And I could intellectually understand that the pain of my childhood had frozen me in time and wholly colored my identity. My little waif shoved her heels into the ground and shook from fear. Though I often fought it, this fear prevented me from stepping out and being heard. Today she was still doing it, though a little less often or in different ways. She and I had been working together for over 14 months, but I often felt she would <u>never</u> feel secure, or ever completely heal. I wanted to forgive… *"Forgive and forget"*, or at least *'let go'*. The past is over, done. Louise Hay, a well-known transformational speaker and author, explains: *"The point of power is in the present moment"*. (1) True. Still, my present moments replayed (on an unconscious level) the burned script of a traumatic, de-personalizing childhood.

> The Course says: *no one can forgive a sin that he believes is real. And what has consequences must be real, because what it has done is here to see.* (2)

How many times had my therapist supported that viewpoint? I had been brutalized as she said in French: *"il y a beaucoup de dégâts"* (*there's a lot of damage*). And, according to *A Course in Miracles*, *"forgiveness is not pity, which but seeks to pardon what it thinks to be the truth.* (ACIM, text, chapter 27, section II line 2.6)

> *Who can say and mean, 'my brother, you have injured me, and yet, because I am the better of the two, I pardon you my hurt'. His pardon and your hurt cannot exist together.*
> *Who forgives is healed. And in his healing lies the proof that he has truly pardoned, and retains no trace of condemnation that he still would hold against himself or any living thing. Forgiveness is not real unless it brings a healing to your brother and yourself. (3)*

Intellectually I could understand this, but not live it. Consequently, repeatedly, events occurred to show me my learning was incomplete, and I continued to hold grievances and judge my life a disaster. I was unable to live the happy, fulfilling life I wanted, and as an excuse I clung desperately to the believed reason: my childhood experiences. How could I let *"the miracle undo all things the world attests can never be undone"*? (ACIM chapter 27.II, line 6.4)

<u>That</u> was the question.

---

(1) The Power is Within You, Louise L. Hay
(2) ACIM text, chapter 27.II.lines 2.4-6
(3) ACIM text, chapter 27. II lines 2.8-9; lines 3.10-4.1

CHAPTER 10

A New Beginning

In place of the constant fear and tension I had experienced most of my life, peace settled and clarity dawned. As I read the opening chapters of the Course, I began to understand. A new name came to me for my book: *Unreasonable Love-the Message of Psychosynthesis and A Course in Miracles*. I could see that psychosynthesis was about love...accepting and loving the whole self, and allowing the transpersonal Self to heal. Like the Course, it seeks to remove the obstacles we have placed to block love's presence. The reclaiming of Self is love; according to *A Course in Miracles* nothing else exists. ACIM begins: "Nothing real can be threatened. Nothing unreal exists. Herein lies the peace of God."(ACIM, Preface "What It Says"). This can be the source of our own peace, if we choose it, and if we free ourselves sufficiently from the grasp of the ego or small self's conditioning.

I had spent the last week in dreadful conflict and anxiety, agonizing over <u>how</u> to respond to, and honor the fighting subpersonalities within me. I could see they had been in conflict for many years. The frightened little waif, the wild, feminine, fiery woman, and the dark, foreboding masculine figure shaking its long skinny finger in my face...these three parts of me, echoes from another time or place, vied for attention, power, and space. Several days ago, I was drawn to the second chapter in the Course, *The Separation and the Atonement*. Section VI is entitled *Fear and Conflict*. It felt perfect...exactly where I was, in fear and conflict. As I read, different sentences leapt out at me:

> When you are fearful, you have chosen wrongly... You must change your mind, not your behavior, and this is a matter of willingness." Line 2.6 clearly states: "The truth is that you are responsible for what you think, because it is only at this level that you can exercise choice. (1)

I understand this concept intellectually, but cannot seem to apply it in life.

Relying on the use of 'will,' Roberto Assagioli and Edgar Cayce corroborate the concept of choice. I continue reading. In the same section, line 6.7 explains:

> *Only your mind can produce fear. It does so whenever it is conflicted in what it wants, producing inevitable strain because wanting and doing are discordant. This can be corrected only by accepting a unified goal. (2)*

"What goal is that?" I ask. The Course continues on line 7.1:

> *The first corrective step in undoing the error is to know first that the conflict is an expression of fear." Line 7.2 explains: Say to yourself that you must somehow have chosen not to love, or the fear could not have arisen.*

Chosen not to love... love whom or what? The paragraph outlines a "series of pragmatic steps" in lines 7.5-8.

> *Know first that this is fear.*
> *Fear arises from lack of love.*
> *The only remedy for lack of love is perfect love.*
> *Perfect love is the Atonement.*

Though I am not totally clear, I feel an opening, like a crack in a thick mental carapace.

> *...when you are afraid, you have placed yourself in a position where you need Atonement. You have done something loveless, having chosen without love. This is precisely the situation for which the Atonement was offered.*

ACIM, T.Chapter 2, sect. VI, lines 8.3-8.5

What does this mean exactly? I feel I need <u>anything</u> to alleviate my conflict and debilitating inability to see clearly and choose differently. I have looked everywhere, listened to tapes, read books, gone through more than a year's work in psychosynthesis study, spent two years in therapy... <u>Still</u> those harsh voices of the past convince me how weak I am, how unworthy, and how disobedient and awful I must be to find myself in my present life circumstances...abandoned and forgotten by husband, lover, family, and professional circles.

Lines 8.6-9: *The need for the remedy inspired its establishment. As long as you recognize only the need for the remedy, you will remain fearful. However, as soon as you accept the remedy, you have abolished the fear. This is how true healing occurs.*

<u>Acceptance</u>. The words of lesson 139: *"I will accept Atonement for myself"* echo in my mind. How many times have I struggled in my mind, believing I accept "at-one-ment" and forgiveness, but in reality not wanting to let go of my judgements and interpretation?

I read a little further.

> *The mind is very powerful, and never loses its creative force. It never sleeps. Every instant it is creating... There are no idle thoughts. All thinking produces form at some level.*
> ACIM, chpt 2, sect. VI lines 9.5-14

The words sink in slowly, as if through thick sludge. The terrible tightness and pain in my chest, the recent painful, stiff neck, the panic within, the feeling of fear and lack of peace... I am **resisting letting go**. I am perpetuating my belief in victimization and resisting change. This possibility has only reinforced a sense of guilt and deeper unworthiness.

I read on in Section VII, *Cause and Effect* (lines 1.1; 1-8):

> *You may still complain about fear, but you persist in making yourself fearful... You may feel that at this point it would take a miracle to enable you to 'guard your thoughts carefully', which is perfectly true.*

I do feel the only way to control my thoughts, which are putting me through such hell is through a miracle (or a lobotomy). Lines 3.1-3.3 state:

> *Both miracles and fear come from thoughts. If you are not free to choose one, you would also not be free to choose the other. By choosing the miracle you have rejected fear...*

What is the miracle but the realization that all the thoughts of death, unworthiness and self-loathing are mere thoughts, having only the power I attribute to them? (3) The feeling and vision I have of a dark, masculine figure pointing an unflinching, accusing finger of guilt: *"how dare you go against the family injunction to "shut up and put up"*... is a mental construct that holds power only as long as I give it power. When I allow this understanding to genuinely take root, I will be free to choose.

> *Nothing and everything cannot coexist. To believe in one is to deny the other. Fear is really nothing and love is everything. Whenever light enters darkness, the darkness is abolished.* **What you believe is true is true for you.** (my bold print)
> (ACIM chapter 2, section VII, lines 5.1-5.5)

The section finishes with the words in lines 7.6-7:

> *Confidence cannot develop fully until mastery has been accomplished. We have already attempted to correct the fundamental error that fear can be mastered, and have emphasized that the only real mastery is through love.*

Pushing against and forcing will not succeed, only a gentle letting go through love.

In the last section of this chapter, the following words concerning the importance of 'will' would be dear to Roberto Assagioli's heart:

> *Since creative ability rests in the mind, everything you create is necessarily a matter of will."* (Section VIII, "The Meaning of the Last Judgment", line 1.4) (4)

It <u>really</u> is up to us. Love is the only enduring answer. Trite it may sound, but within me a recurring knowing persists… like the refrain in one of Loreena McKennit's songs: *"love must make us strong."*

Amid the pain, suffering, and fear we feel, we must learn to focus on what we **truly** desire. Do we want death, horror, conflict, hatred, suffering? Or, do we want the miracle of love, gentleness and peace? Is not our very essence love and kindness as Piero Ferrucci affirms in a talk on "kindness," given at the Psychosynthesis and Education Trust in London, and in his book *The Power of Kindness?* (5)

Is this world really an illusion as the Course instructs (ACIM lesson 155 line 2) and as many Eastern philosophies explain? Are we merely asleep, dreaming a dreadful nightmare of abuse, hatred, anger, and fear? (6) Suppose we **are** kind, and our essence **is** love, yet we are afraid, afraid we are guilty of some unspeakable sin… The fear of retribution drives us, the fear of some terrible sin, so we dare not look within, and instead, spend our time in useless seeking without for something to "save us."

> *Seek not outside yourself. For it will fail, and you will weep each time an idol falls.* (ACIM chapter 29, The Awakening, section VII *Seek Not Outside Yourself;* Lines 1.1-2)

I knew about that. I had wanted A. and other men in my past to save me from the anguish of deep-rooted unworthiness and guilt. Naturally, the unconscious plan had failed. And now, instead of hiding, I had come face to face with my own terrifying fear of unworthiness and an unbearable hatred projected out.

Today I wanted to see differently. The Course asks: *"Do you prefer that you be right or happy?"* (Chapter 29 sect VII, line 1.9) Despite our fear, we <u>must</u> choose kindness and we must choose <u>love</u>. In spite of my ego's loud clamoring to the contrary, I preferred to be happy, and I preferred to discover a "path of the heart," a path of gentleness and non-violence. What 'will' do we possess other than to choose to be who we truly are?

The Course explains its aim is not to teach love, but to teach us to remove the obstacles and blocks we have erected against love. Lesson 153 teaches: "*In my defenselessness my safety lies.*" This lesson explains how we are slave to the *"sense of threat the world encourages."*

> *Attack, defense; defense, attack become the circles of the hours and the days that bind the mind in heavy bands of steel with iron overlaid, returning but to start again. There seems to be no break nor ending in the ever-tightening grip of the imprisonment upon the mind.* (ACIM lesson 153 Lines 3.2-3)

How accurate this feels; we need but look around us everyday to find "proof" of how weak and vulnerable we believe we are, and how dangerous the world is. Turn on the news at any hour of the day in any country for further corroboration. Yet, Piero Ferrucci prefers to believe we are <u>kind</u>. How we use our will is up to us…to give credence to the ego's play of righteous anger and victimization, or, to realize our potential of love, kindness, and peace.

> *Sin is the home of all illusions, which but stand for things imagined, issuing from thoughts that are untrue. They are the "proof" that what has no reality is real. Sin "proves" God's Son is evil; timelessness must have an end; eternal life must die. …*
>
> *A madman's dreams are frightening, and sin appears indeed to terrify. And yet what sin perceives is but a childish game…*
>
> *How long, O Son of God, will you maintain the game of sin? Shall we not put away these sharp-edged children's toys? How soon will you be ready to come home? Perhaps today?* (ACIM workbook Part II.4, *What is Sin?* Lines 3.1-5.4)

* * *

For three days I have suffered from what in French is called "*torticolis*," an incapacitating tightness in my neck. The pain keeps me from turning my head to the right or from lying down without sharp, agonizing pain shooting through my head. Symbolic deciphering of this physical ailment informs me it is related to *"a feeling or inability to say 'no' to a situation".* (7) How "*à propos*", since it arrived the very morning after I said "no" to the family injunction and duty to be "professional, responsible, and to GROW UP". I sent an email to my sister saying I was not ready to come to the U.S. for Christmas, not wanting to give up my insecure "bohemian" lifestyle in the countryside in France. I felt I needed the quiet and unstructured existence I had in France to finish my book, and I wanted to wait for a possible job I desired in Biarritz to play out. Unfortunately (or maybe not) the end of year holidays had put a hold on interviewing, and I needed to wait until the beginning of the New Year to see if I was called for an interview.

This morning I realized the pain in my neck was a message to let go of the tightness. There was no need to fight by saying, "no". I could let go, trust my true essence to speak and guide me. The guidance would be clear once I removed the resistance and feeling of upset. I felt more peaceful. I had spoken. I had spoken from my true Self and I had expressed a personal desire that went against my father's dictates and commands. I had done it.

---

(1) ACIM, Text, chapter 2. Sect. VI, line 3.2-3.4; line 2.6
(2) ACIM T. chapter 2 sect VI lines 6.7-9
(3) See ACIM Text, Chapter 2 The Separation and the Atonement, sections VI § VII
(4) For an in-depth discussion of will, refer to Assagioli, *The Act of Will*
(5) Piero Ferrucci, *The Power of Kindness*, Penguin books 2007
(6) Buddhist and Hindu teachings also speak of "Maya" or "Samsara", the world of illusion, to be overcome in favor of truth.
(7) Translated from Michel Odoul, *Dis-moi où tu as mal (Le lexique)*

Trust and Flow

Saturday October 18th

I awoke with no plans, but felt calm. Finally I can feel calm, have no plans, no people to see and a void or question mark on my life's agenda. I had gone to a concert the night before to hear Manu Di Bango, an artist I'd wanted to hear since a diplomat friend, musician and friend of Manu's, had spoken of him in New York. That was 30 years ago. And here he was playing one night, a mere 40-minute drive away, in rural France.

Everything was organized last minute...the tickets opened up 'magically.' A friend, Philippe, was available to accompany me and off we went. The concert was exquisite, fabulous jazz with African overtones. A full house, we were in standing room, but it was perfect to move to the music and share a moment of communion with other people, enjoying the vibrant life and energy that music weaves into people's beings. Pure magic! Philippe and I had not eaten dinner before the concert, so we wandered out afterwards, wondering if we would find a restaurant that served at 11 p.m.; remember this is a quiet, rural part of France.

As if guided, we stumbled onto a lit-up restaurant in the medieval part of town that announced it served late. When we went inside the owner told us he was awaiting the musicians themselves... I just knew it! The meal was delicious and time with Philippe pleasant. After so much aloneness, it felt refreshing to share with another human being, even if our motivations and desires in life were different. Like most healthy, red-blooded Frenchmen, Philippe wished our relationship to take a more intimate turn, but this evening he exerted no pressure, and wished me a respectful *goodnight* when the evening drew to a close at 2 a.m.

The evening was perfect and easy. I did little to put the pieces in place, other than to plant two seeds: a phone call to the theatre and a passing comment to Philippe. More and more, I could see my life unfold in this manner – no pushing, striving, or struggling. A professional teaching opportunity in Paris had recently come my way in a similar manner. What at first seemed an unlikely eventuality had come together in a way that responded to both my needs and my requests.

Despite these responses to my needs, I doubted...perhaps not always, but I felt myself holding on to a belittling, negative voice, that said: *"it won't happen this time...that was just a fluke...things don't work out for you...why should they? Who the hell are you anyway?"*

This Saturday morning, after sleeping in with Brownie, I felt like company during breakfast, and decided to turn on my portable computer where I had downloaded a number of personal development seminars. I had already listened to most of them, but something nudged me to get the computer out anyway. Maybe there were one or two programs I had not listened to, or maybe I would be inspired to listen again to one I had not heard in awhile. I saw a file entitled '*Marianne*,' and clicked on it, wondering what it could be (in my mind making a connection to the symbolic name for France). But that was not at all the subject of this talk... In midstream a workshop began by Marianne Williamson. *

Her words were on target, exactly where I found myself in my own life classroom tutorial. Uncanny it is how God, or the Knowing of the Universe seems to be present at the right time, with the right teaching, the right message. It was and **is**, totally mysterious.

Marianne Williamson's seminar this morning came a week after I had had a dream image of a catamaran... cutting the rope to a heavy weight, and feeling the boat instantly shoot forth with speed and purpose. Shortly after that, I had been toying with the theme for my monthly coaching newsletter. Then, in receiving a request from a potential client, the theme became clear: *"Relâchez le lest et foncez!"* *"Release the ballast and GO!"*

Intellectually I understood, knowing that the emotional exploring and cleaning out I had been doing for over a year, now needed releasing. Still, something held me back. *What was it?* Fear. Of standing out (or up) and being counted? I felt I had identified a 'mission' or purpose in life...and was fulfilling it, quietly. I was not shouting it out at the top of my lungs, perhaps for fear of being heard too much. A part of me was afraid I would not manage numerous coaching clients or seminars, and too many people. How would I manage if a successful and busy coach? I needed time to meditate, sleep, and take care of myself...no one else did that now that I was alone. Wasn't the whole message of healing, that I needed to give myself the love, attention and care I had never received in life? No more waiting for Prince Charming or someone else to do things for me – **I** had to be independent and capable!

I <u>was</u> pleased with what I was able to accomplish lately, things I never thought myself capable of doing before. Today with time and patience, taking one step at a time, I managed life without feeling paralysed, out of control or terrorized. I had even become accustomed to driving places alone, calmly, without panic…navigating my way through unknown places, sitting alone in restaurants or other public places, without feeling the weight of heavy judgment and criticism that admonished: *"YOU don't belong to the human race, or you wouldn't be alone."*

Today, I could actually spend much time alone, and be at peace. I could <u>choose</u> to be alone, instead of with someone whose energy depleted me or did not interest me. I had come a <u>long</u> way, a very long way for me, and I was pleased with myself. I had heard the internal call of Self, and I was beginning to awaken.

---

* Marianne Williamson is an author and internationally acclaimed lecturer on *A Course in Miracles*

Care and Safety

To respond to the call to be oneself, to **be** regardless of others' judgments or reactions…to truly live and create…you need to feel safe. It has to feel safe to come out of hiding and I could see this was crucial for me. I could also see how a part of me was unsure how safe it really was.

As a child it had never been safe. There had been a lot of pretence about family and what's "*good for you*", but it had never been safe to be who you were. How was the terrified part of me, cut down and castigated, was she to be sure that today it was safe?

As an exercise, my therapist suggested I think of a place where neither parent could enter. For me this needed to be a place where no family member could enter, a place where my little girl could be safe, come out of hiding, be herself, and in a sense, be born. As I mused on this idea, a comical image came to me: French President Nicholas Sarkozy holding up a hand to stop my father, mother, and sister from alighting on French soil, explaining that only **I** had the right to enter France. I smiled as I viewed this imaginary scene. In a way, how true it was! They could not get me in France, nor make me leave. I could see with hindsight how I had run away, fled across the Atlantic to a foreign country, learned to speak the language like a native, and created a new personality. I had even been "christened" in France with my official name, *Olivia*. (1)

Today I could see the unconscious symbolism, and strongly felt the need to heal the wound. I no longer wanted to live in exile. In short, I was feeling a pull to return to the U.S., or at least to live and work with Americans.

My imagined image of the highest symbol of French law (the President) protecting me and creating a safe haven was both humorous and true. But, as Mme F. pointed out, it was insufficient. I needed strength and a force that came from **within,** and that strength or force, I did not feel. As my therapist and I explored this together in an interior journey, I saw myself as a small person on a very small surfboard, trying to surf an enormous wave in Hawaii, saying to myself: "*I don't know how to surf.*"

That is the way life felt most of the time, like an enormous wave in a frightening land of large, powerful waves… and me, terrified, on a very small surfboard, not knowing how to surf...wondering how I was going to manage. I remembered a similar image during the psychosynthesis class in London two years ago, and the feeling of a powerful whirlpool spinning downward, dragging me with it.

Today, despite my deep work and exploration, I was not being dragged under, but was still not feeling safe or in control. Was I ever going to feel capable of managing my own life? Would I ever feel secure, rid myself of the family injunction to be incapable, useless, and a failure?

I felt pretty incapable and inept at the game of life and it is this feeling I had sought to escape in running away to a foreign country. Inside I truly felt "*nulle*"(null). Mme F. reassured me that given the childhood circumstances, it had had to be that way. She said as a child, I had no choice but to obey the family injunction in order to survive.

During this interior journey with Mme F., my eyes closed, my hands involuntarily moved up to cover my eyes, and I said: *"she couldn't see what was happening."* How true. I couldn't see it. "I" or "she" had gone numb...dead. The word *'morteresse'* came out of my mouth. I said this to Mme F., knowing it is not a real French word. She responded by saying: *"of course, this little girl could not do more than what she did; she <u>had</u> to be 'morteresse'* (dead-like, numb, asleep, not really alive) *so Olivia could survive."* Mme F. said: *"thank her for all that she did to keep you alive, to allow Olivia to survive".* Silently I did as she suggested, and almost immediately saw in my mind's eye an old crone in a dark basement, stirring a cauldron of dark and ominous liquid. I had encountered this crone during my first week of psychosynthesis work in London so long ago... at that time she had appeared in the cellar of a house I was exploring in a meditation. (2)

In today's vision, my little girl was peering down and around from the top of the stairway leading to the dark cellar. She was afraid of the ugly old woman and whatever else might be lurking in the dank, dark cellar. I could "see" this scene and how strange it appeared as I looked on, my eyes covered with my own hands. I became aware and amazed at this little girl, who had half-died, become frozen and *'morteresse,'* sacrificing herself in becoming small and voiceless, so I could live.

Subsequently, as if someone communicated new information to me, I realized it was the crone, the old woman, who had made the potion that made little Olivia *'morteresse'*...that put her to sleep, half-dead. The realization hit me hard: this part of me had also saved me. This archetypal crone (3) knew a secret recipe or potion so Olivia would be dead without dying, and sleep while still waking. She had made little Olivia *'morteresse.'* The crone no longer appeared terrifying...she had corroborated to save me. The question today became: **Is it still necessary to remain half dead, numb and asleep in life?**

* * *

As I relaxed into the reverie and let my imagination carry me, the old crone became younger...a slim, lithe woman, wearing a tight, black, high-necked, dress with long, draped sleeves. She was still in the cellar, which I now noticed had shelves against the walls, supporting dark unlabeled bottles; it looked like an old apothecary. This apothecary did not have traditionally shaped bottles, for these were all gracefully shaped – sensuous, rounded and flowing, made of beautiful blown glass of rich, deep opaque colors: deep wine red and rich dark blues and blacks. The beautiful, svelte, wise woman knew what each bottle (though unlabeled) contained, and knew what concoction to create. I was sure she could make me a potion to protect myself, to be strong. **She** would know an exact blend of herbs, powders and fluids, and no one else would ever know the recipe.

Almost as soon as this thought entered my mind and I began to relax, a moment of fear followed. Could I **really** trust this crone/sorcerer? What if she were like my father...fickle, playing kind and caring, only to change shape suddenly once the protective potion was no longer active to keep me safe in a numbed, deadened, protected state? As if in answer, I saw an outdoor fire, a circle of light and warmth in the dark. At a distance from the fire, just out of reach of the light were wolves... I could see their bright eyes reflected in the fire. The graceful, slim dark woman in black, with one quiet downward gesture of her arms, made the wolves lie down. She mesmerized them, making them totally obedient and tame. And I, feeling light and carefree, realized I could dance in the warm, playful circle of light around the dancing flames of the fire. I felt a desire to dance naked around and round, to sing and be joyful, without thought or judgment of any kind: <u>to just be</u>. I recalled later, during the second day of my women's workshop, entitled "*le Sacré Féminin*", (The Sacred Feminine) two days before my therapy session, out of nowhere I had felt an urge to dance flamenco. Yet, I do not know how to dance flamenco…

(1) Several months after I had been introduced in France through official immigration channels for a job in Paris, my direct superior had asked if I minded being called by my first name? This was an honor in a country where informality is rarely used; secondly, it was unusual to hear my true name voiced since 'at home' a nickname had always been used.
(2) The image of a house is a common symbolic message for the exploration of self, with the cellar or basement symbolizing the unconscious.
(3) See Caroline Myss, *Sacred Contracts* for more information on archetypes and their messages.

CHAPTER 11

Lost in Incarnation,
or Here we go again...

Back to "reality." My chest hurts. I feel sad, <u>so sad</u>, abandoned and alone. It may be illusion as the Course instructs, mere phenomena, as Ram Dass teaches, not who I really am, far from my true essence, but I <u>experience</u> and feel great fear and aloneness. *What is to become of me?*

I feel like I am dancing on the edge of a bottomless abyss, and I will fall, fall into the void...to more pain, more emotional and physical disarray and discombobulation. My little waif who I now call *Morteresse*, is afraid, mortally terrified. She and I screwed up all our courage and made the decision despite the loneliness, **not** to fly to the U.S. this Christmas. Something unidentifiable within kept gnawing, groaning, and <u>resisting</u>. A recurrent voice inside repeated over and over, while I experienced deep dread:

> *It is impossible for you to go to a non life-supporting environment with 'rules' that you do not believe in, which (for you) restrict and remove lightness, fun and relaxation; it is impossible now that you have come so far and experienced what knocks you off balance.*

My heart hurts too much. I feel the image of a wounded, bleeding blob with no skin to protect it from the sun, writhing on a hot sidewalk. A passer-by would want to kick it aside, so gross and unpleasant is it to see. The blob throbs with some life, but is raw, oozing and agonizing in the hot sun, with hardly any hope of healing. As I write, sobbing begins, like an uncontrollable retching from my chest, and tears flood my screwed up eyes.

<u>*How much do I have to cry?*</u> How long do I have to feel this pain, and review again and again my family's cold, uncaring abandonment? I clearly see their actions today as an inability to love, or love in a way I need. Only yesterday, another innocent Sunday phone call from my sister smacked another stab in my chest.

My heart aches; it bleeds. In pain I sit alone in the countryside in France in an effort to protect and mend my oozing, bleeding heart. This must be the reason for my enforced "exile;" I cannot seem to let the pain go. *"Just let it go"*, my sister authoritatively suggests;" *it's over, learn what you need and move on…"* Excellent advice, but I can't do it, no matter how much I look at the neglect, craziness, abuse, and justification for survival personality, "explanations" from the past. No matter how I have prayed to move on, pain and paralysing fear rear their heads like Cerberus, the three-headed dog at the entrance to Hades. Unsuspecting, they hit me from an unseen angle in another form of attack, abandonment and reinforced guilt, almost as if to say: *"you made your bed, now lie in it."*

Yesterday, a mere 6 days after I reimbursed my plane ticket, my sister called to say she had found someone to housesit when she leaves mid-January for her new job. I said that was "great," repeating several times during the conversation that I had no problem staying in the house with this woman, if my job option in Biarritz fell through and I decided to come to the U.S. in January. It seemed when we had spoken a week ago we had left the situation open for me to come to Washington in a few months, once I finished writing and had explored the potential job in Biarritz. Now it felt like I was "out to lunch." As the conversation unfolded, it became clear someone else had priority over my sister's house in Washington. This new woman was not to pay rent, but she was not expecting anyone else in the house, my sister assured me. With three bedrooms, still my sister could not hear the possibility or option of two of us sharing the house. I felt like a rug had been pulled out from under my feet, again. I didn't seem to have anything secure from family to depend upon.

I was surprised and stunned once again. As the conversation continued, my sister talked about the guidance I was receiving, clearly indicating I needed to stay in France, at least for the moment. (I wondered if her idea of "moment" and mine were not diametrically different). She explained how my email had expressed reticence at a regular job, and how I had a trickle of income in France… All in all, she kept trying to tell me what I had said (instead of letting me express myself) and underlined several times that I had changed my mind about coming. Yes, I <u>had</u> emailed her saying I was not ready. And we had spoken, and she had encouraged me to trust my intuition, so I had asked for the reimbursement and paid the penalty. In so doing,

I had experienced a nagging panic, but had done it, and felt it was right. I experienced great sorrow, wishing things were different in our family, as illustrated in a chapter I wrote of a new, "true" fairy tale, entitled *Morteresse**, but **I had done it.**

After yesterday's upset and gripping fear at the thought of being cut off from "home" in America, my panic showed me the tangled vines of fear, firmly rooted in my mind. I kept insisting this fear was my family's fault, the reason I was afraid in life and anxious to survive. As I sat with heavy pain in my chest Sunday morning, I realized I was still "playing the game", caught. I based my inability to live the way <u>I wanted to live</u>, on my parents and my abusive childhood…lack of love and psychological abandonment. My weakness and fear clearly seemed to be **their** fault, my family's responsibility for not loving me and for piercing my heart with rejection! That had to be the cause of the heaviness and constant pain in my chest. Yet, through this thought, another one arose. Was **I**, as an adult, perpetuating the story through blame, being sure it was someone else's fault? *After all these years, is my family responsible for my life at 51?*

A part of me wanted to leave France, to go "home" to show I was healed, no longer affected by the sorrow, anger, and loss of my past, no longer waif-like, sad, and unhappy. This part of me was still fighting against the past, wanting to show up as a responsible adult who lived in society, made a good living, no longer scrambling for wood to heat a little house in the woods because she felt wounded and fearful of humanity. The need to **prove** something revealed the ego dynamic described in the Course, and the belief in "not being good enough," imprinted as a child. I was still milking my victimization story for all its worth, while the hidden reality of the game was unloving disapproval of <u>myself.</u>

My ego pushed me to <u>prove</u> the right to happiness, peace, and the right to exist. This part of me hated **me**. I was experiencing in my own life the vicious ego dynamic the Course describes in great length. The concept of my "self" had accepted a soap opera drama the Course explains as a way to veil our true essence and our light… in short, our potential and greatness. For me (as for all of us) my own life story was truth; in my version, I could not measure up, was guilty, and must continue to "pay". Camouflaged in the sticky web of ego games and projection, I hated and disapproved of myself. On a hidden, unconscious level, a part of me agreed to and authored a horrific story of diminished self, objectification, and abuse that continued long after I remained in the original circumstances. An innocent victim, I was not to blame, but my family certainly was.

This is the classic story of projection *A Course in Miracles* explains, the ego's tactic to push the blame of a dissatisfying or hopeless life, (where the "hero/heroine" of the dream is an innocent victim) onto a responsible, unloving, and vile party. I needed to keep the story alive since it served me. Despite renewed disappointments with family, I kept trying, a bit like banging your head against a wall… something apparently I did in my crib as a baby. I hoped against hope, expecting my family to "*be there*" for me. I wanted my family to respond in what I considered "normal", loving and supportive responses. And I was continually disappointed to find they were unable to love the way I wanted them to.

It had always been the case that to receive support and approval I was expected to abide by and respect strict principles, what I called 'rules.' Abiding by those rules depressed me and dampened my joy and energy. But because I felt so lost and alone, I kept going back in search of family and love, but when I could not accept and feel good in the restrictive environment, I condemned myself as "*useless*" or "*incapable.*" Alone in the world after my divorce, I felt if I disobeyed family beliefs, I risked being "*chased from the garden*", "*thrown out of the tribe*" or ostracized, and "*left to the wolves.*" In many ways this is what I had experienced in childhood, so I was already "*out of the tribe.*"

* * *

It is almost noon. I have not eaten breakfast or showered. I no longer experience guilt when I can't get going in the morning. I accept my own rhythm – that's just the way it is. It is winter. I do not work regularly, so my schedule is quite free. I heat my little house with wood and in the morning, the house being cold and dark, I find it hard to extricate myself from my warm bed, so I remain in quiet warmth and safety. This is a way of being gentle and kind to myself, allowing myself this luxury and sweetness. I often awake during the night and write about awareness or understandings that dawn on me, born out of darkness and silence.

At noon, I stop writing to eat breakfast. As I eat my toast, I realize it is three days to Christmas. I have not contacted any friends. I need to if I do not want to experience heavy solitude, yet a part of me has no desire to be with people, particularly those who lack genuine kindness and gentleness. I cannot bear the game that "all is well," when I am filled with sadness. My queen subpersonality judges this reaction "silly", to still be grieving a family I never had… but there it is. I feel it is more frustrating to have a family that pretends to be caring, than to have lost one's family long ago to death and definitive departure. At least in the latter case, they are gone, and one is <u>family-less</u>. I feel family-less, yet by appearance I have a family. So, what am I grieving? Why do I isolate myself? People do not understand, and no one speaks of it. I have found most people do not know how to be with sadness and grief; they would rather not know. Perhaps that human frailty or failure is a godsend in disguise.

How many people have a family that truly supports and understands them? Maybe not as many as I believe… In any case, I am the one who thinks about my story. And if I do not release it somehow, we will go around and around again, adding twists on the story line, but maintaining the same vein, the same play of sadness, abandonment and victimization. I will remain "lost in incarnation."

(*) <u>Morteresse</u> is the name of a fairy tale, a modern version of *Sleeping Beauty* I am writing for children.

CHAPTER 12

Holiday Teachings

Christmas Eve

It is the day before Christmas. In France this is the big day or evening I should say: the "*reveillon.*" Yesterday in the streets of Cahors, people were shopping in great preparation. The stores were crowded as shoppers bought last minute presents, and stocked up on traditional goodies and foodstuffs for the "*reveillon*" dinner.

I was pleased to be part of the bustle in town yesterday, for today I am alone in my little house in the woods. Yet, as I write, I do not feel lonely this bright and sunny, cold day. I have my book, which is becoming more and more a living entity; I have Brownie, and my safe little house that protects me from the cold. Inside, I am secure in a warm cocoon where a birthing is taking place. I awoke this morning with a far off feeling of getting close to something intangible, but real. I even feel a sense of gratitude for my crazy family! Without them and my past experiences, I would not understand the symbolism of where I am in life. Perhaps I am still resisting what I see, not totally wanting to accept a possible truth, but a part of me now knows that what the majority of people believe and live by, is <u>not true</u>.

As a child, my father often repeated to me stories I was to tell at school, if anyone asked… I could see these was untrue, and often so crazy that they laid the groundwork for my ability to see through a life story. Today, like the awakening of *Morteresse* in my fairy tale, similar to an understanding I felt standing on the bridge in the little village of Castelfranc, <u>this</u> awakening is up to *Morteresse*, i.e. me. We cannot expect a sorceress or anyone else to choose for us – we alone can decide to awaken. This is the foundation teaching of the Course. Each of us (alone) must decide to accept Atonement, or what the Course professes as *"the natural profession of the children of God,"* (1) for ourselves.

Two days ago I awoke with a hazy question: *"and if I were **wrong**?"* What if the pain I feel around my heart is not a reflection of family neglect and abuse, with me as a poor, wronged martyr? What if that story hides another story too immensely frightening to look at, a story concocted to veil an existential hatred and feeling of guilt? The Course explains in great detail the ego's game to bury the cause of deep, uncontrollable guilt and the root of "the authority problem." My perpetuation of misery, sadness, and a recurrent belief in not being able to survive, are forms of self-loathing and hatred. Today, my parents are no longer responsible for me. My aged, arthritic father is in no position to inflict physical abuse, and any emotional abuse is only what I am willing to accept.

In my most recent relationship with A, **I** accepted his *"on again, off again"* treatment of me. I allowed him to play the game that ultimately led to abandonment. I did not want to see how he had no intention of honoring his promise to leave his wife and family contract. He entertained his own dream, and was caught in his own illusions. The question was not his guilt at leading me on; it was my desire to be mistreated and blind. In the end I could point the figure of innocent accusation and say: "*Behold me brother, at your hand I die.*" (2)

My childhood story, on a deeper level, reflected the same dynamic. Though resistant, a part of me was beginning to see it. Today, without my story, I would be free, yet I could not let it go. In some respects my ego reminded me of Lady Macbeth, repeating over and over how sad and righteous I had the right to feel. "*I fear the lady doth protest too much.*" Why not "*let sleeping dogs lie*" and move on? Why was I still experiencing the painful twisting of a symbolic sword in my heart as if every experience in life was an excuse to point out how *bad, undeserving,* or *unwanted* a being I was? What did my sister's decision to choose a total stranger to housesit her house have to do with me? I had said I was not coming… I could see how my pain and upset always revolved around the same point of departure: an abused, uncared-for, tortured little waif I had named Morteresse…and her story of abandonment. I could glimpse my own ego in action.

What was the payoff? What was the point of spinning such a torturous, unhappy story for one's life? The Course explains that beneath all life stories, the ego's real motivation is hatred, though it covers this through the "face of innocence" and seeks someone else to blame.

> *For what can specialness delight in but to kill? What does it seek for but the sight of death? Where does it lead but to*

destruction? Yet think not that it looked upon your brother first, nor hated him before it hated you. The sin its eyes behold in him and love to look upon it saw in you...(3)

Workbook Lesson 79 explains: *Let me recognize the problem so it can be solved.* And what is the problem? Despite appearances of a multitude of problems in our lives, *A Course in Miracles* says we have only one... and that is a belief in separation. As I ask quietly, what is the problem, my eyes shoot open with the response: "the desire to be right".

Christmas Day

« *I walk with God in perfect holiness.* » (ACIM, workbook lesson 156)

What a freeing idea and thought! I do want to believe it on Christmas day.

I walk with God in perfect holiness.
Who walks with me? (4)

The lesson suggests we ask this question a thousand times a day until certainty replaces doubt...so today, Christmas day, despite appearances, I affirm I am not alone. And the perfect gift this Christmas day is the following thought:

There is no cause for guilt and being causeless, does not exist (line 2). ....*ideas leave not their source. If this be true how can you be apart from God? How could you walk the world alone and separate from your Source?"* (Lines 3-4)

I am an idea in the mind of God, and being part of God, *"where He is, there must be Holiness, as much as life."* (Line 3) This is the reason I cannot be alone, abandoned, or unworthy. *"I walk with God in perfect holiness".* Within me *"is a light which cannot die."* (Line 4) The limited, weak way I have seen myself all these years is not who I really am.

The day is white, frosty, crisp, and clean. Today is a new start. The lesson says the light heralds the end of punishment and death, since sin (or mistake) is gone.

In lightness and in laughter is sin gone, because its quaint absurdity is seen. It is a foolish thought, a silly dream, not frightening, ridiculous perhaps, but who would waste an instant in approach to God Himself for such a senseless whim? (Lines 6.4-5)

Yet you have wasted many, many years on just this foolish thought. The past is gone, with all its fantasies. <u>*They keep you bound no longer.*</u> *(My underlined emphasis) The approach to God is near.* (Lines 7.1-4)

Today let doubting cease. God speaks for you in answering your question with these words:

I walk with God in perfect holiness. I light the world, I light my mind and all the minds which God created one with me. (Lines 8.3-6)

With these words to support me, I feel light, relieved, free, and ready to move on in life with grace and ease. The day after tomorrow I leave for Biarritz to follow my "dancer's" inspiration to explore flamenco, and to take myself on my first vacation alone…without boyfriend, girlfriend or other human companion. Brownie, my ever-faithful companion and guardian will naturally accompany me.

The Day after Christmas

I awake late, memories of the night before at the restaurant where I celebrated Christmas with a couple of friends, far away. Today is a day of solitude and quiet, as well as preparation for my departure for Biarritz to explore the area and dance flamenco. I go downstairs to relight my fire and feel snow in the air, the day after Christmas in Southwest France where it snows (or snowed) rarely. I bring in wood, and have barely relit the fire and ensconced myself on the couch, before the snow is falling slowly but surely.

My lesson today offers:

This is a day of silence and of trust. It is a special time of promise in your calendar of days. (5)

I feel a sense of imminence, as if these words have been written exclusively for me. I feel a page turning in slow motion, but the page is being turned. My past is settling into quiet and rest, like in the sands of the ocean, and I feel "I" am emerging, an "I" previously unknown to others and to myself. As I read on, the Course tells me:

This day is holy, for it ushers in a new experience; a different kind of feeling and awareness. You have spent long days and nights in celebrating death. Today you learn to feel the joy of life. (ACIM lesson 157 lines 1.4-6)

As I look out at the quiet and total whiteness, no sound of human life present, I am filled with a bubbling excitement, a sense of expectancy, and a certainty that joy is true. Later, as I write these words, I am listening to music entitled, *Fairy Heart Magic* (5) and again a hushed bubbling of happiness gurgles within me. I somehow know magic is present and I am leaving the darkness behind; how, I do not know, but certain am I to be moving on.

(1) ACIM, text -1 sect. III line 1.10
(2) ACIM, text - 27. I 4:6
(3) ACIM, text- 24 sect V. lines 4.3-7
(4) ACIM workbook lesson 156, line 8
(5) ACIM workbook lesson 157 line1
(6) Composed by Gary Stadler, produced by Sequoia Records www.sequoiarecords.com

CHAPTER 13

An Unplanned Change of Plans

Car Crash

We think we are in control of life. We plan, position and finagle things so they work out the way we want, hopefully. Sometimes they do, and sometimes...they don't.

I was proud of myself. I had organized a break in Biarritz on the Atlantic coast, five days of private flamenco class and a studio apartment...all on a shoestring budget! My desire to dance flamenco had developed in the last few months, an urge felt during my women's workshop, *Le Sacré féminin,* as well as in images and visions on the train, as I went back and forth to Paris to teach. I felt my subpersonality, "the dancer", inspired and alive, screaming to express herself.

Once on the train, rocked by its momentum and supported by the quiet of people in their own personal worlds, I visualized an entire passionate ballet. Listening to flamenco music, I saw myself dancing to a backdrop of projected images of great, wild animals running and living in their natural environment. The power was magnificent and I felt elated, ecstatic and happy.

Because I wanted to allow myself expression, I decided to explore this new track. I adore dance, and had already encountered my "dancer" in tango, tap dancing and lindy hop, but never flamenco. In my vision on the train, I saw waves crashing majestically on a beach the other side of large glass windows in a room where my "dancer" expressed her passion and fire through flamenco. For two years I had also been drawn to Biarritz. I had had the good fortune to deliver training at the European headquarters of the American sportswear company, Quiksilver, and had LOVED the area! I felt at home, energized, and excited. What more amazing turn of events then to find a flamenco teacher willing to give private lessons over the Christmas holidays, and to find a last minute, discounted rental studio for the same week, all in BIARRITZ!

So, Saturday, two days after my quiet Christmas, Brownie and I were off! I had prepared everything we might need or want in the little studio…spices, homemade soup, Brownie's bed, sheets and towels… I packed fun flamenco clothes with a pair of tap shoes (minus the taps). By 10: 30 a.m. we were loaded in the car and carefully driving out over the snow. The snow had not melted as much as I would have liked, and I knew the initial roads would be treacherous due to the ice and curves. In this part of France hardly a straight road exists, and many people would have been unaccustomed to yesterday's heavy snowfall; as such there was a good chance the shaded roads where the sun did not reach would be very icy.

Icy they were. I drove carefully and slowly through several windy patches, slick and slippery. I was a bit nervous, but confident I could do this, and the going would be easier once I left the *Lot département*, and reached more trafficked areas. I had only gone 10 or 12 kilometres, before going around a curve, I either skidded or hit the ice in trying to avoid an oncoming car over the line… I don't know, it all happened so fast. I turned the wheel quickly, knowing I had to go slowly since the back wheels could skid out of control, which they did. I tried to turn the car the opposite way, lost control, fortunately missed the oncoming car…and barrelled into the ditch. I couldn't believe it… grounded! Shaken, but not hurt, I saw several cars stop to help and get me out of the car. Brownie was miraculously unscathed – he was on the passenger side that took the brunt of the crash. A gentleman from Paris heading home with his entire family, waited with me until help arrived about 30 minutes later. My car was towed away and a dour neighbor, rather sulkily, brought Brownie, my bags, suitcase, dog bed, and me…back home. As they dropped me with my goods and chattels unceremoniously on my front stoop, the curtain descended on the "Biarritz Flamenco Escapade" for the end of December 2008.

The Learning Thereof

Needless to say I was shaken up, but I did not expect the crying and upset that followed from my "waif/poor-me" subpersonality. That part of me felt devastated by the uncompassionate neighbor/friend who left me as soon as she could, as well as by the response of another friend I had called while I was sitting with the Parisian gentleman. Unlike this total stranger, who had a 6-7 hour car trip ahead of him back to Paris, but who insisted on not leaving me alone, my "friend" lived less than 10 miles away and was on holiday; he shocked me by responding to my call for help with: "*feeling a bit sick*" and consequently not wishing to come out!

I was stunned. I had just had an accident! My car was in a ditch sideways and I was stuck, trembling on the side of the road with loads of stuff, my vacation ended before beginning. In retrospect, I suppose my little "waif" couldn't bear the lack of caring and abandonment again, particularly from supposed friends. Still, we experienced kindness from the Parisian "angel", and we were O.K., both Brownie and me. Despite this godsend, throughout the afternoon my tears flowed, and I felt very sorry for myself once again. I felt "damned", "marked", "branded," "unworthy" and undeserving of happiness or normal life like other people… other people who get vacation, families, love, and attention. It even felt when I stand up brave and tall, alone, and give myself what I do not receive from others, I am doomed to failure. I felt fragile, shaken, and sad.

In my desperate need for attention I called my sister in America, who was afraid I was badly hurt. When it became clear both Brownie and I were OK, she repeated how grateful I should be. The accident had happened near home, I was unscathed and so was Brownie. I had gotten help, though not from the people I expected. She felt something in the universe wanted to stop me in my tracks and keep me where I was, and obviously there was a lesson for me to learn… "*Yuck! Yes, O.K., but **where was the sympathy and care I wanted?**"* It was there, but not in the way I wanted it. So, I pulled myself together, called the insurance company, contacted the studio I had rented, who offered no refund of any kind, and allowed my achy body to rest, as the shock began to settle in.

By the next day, after a long and heavy sleep, my body ached, but I realized I was O.K. and so was Brownie. He could have been killed from the shock; after all it was on his side, and he wears no seatbelt. But all was well, other than the car. Still, I felt numb to gratitude, and could see my mind replaying the well-worn video… "*Here we go again, another thing I try that does not work out, another problem and I am all alone…*" I could hear the well-known voice of my childhood waif and angry little girl: "*this is just not possible… somebody has to help me, somebody has to take care of me!*" Yesterday, during our phone conversation, my sister had mentioned the book, *The Celestine Prophesy*, twice. In this book by James Redfield, there are nine lessons or key insights into life. The first, my sister remembered, had to do with self-pity. When she mentioned this I was half listening. I had read the book over 10 years ago and was sure my ex-husband had taken it with him when he left; besides I could not hear my own self-pity, for I felt righteous in my injury and need for attention.

But, before going to bed I felt an urge to look at the bottom shelf of a small bookcase on the side of the bed where my husband had slept. Lo and behold, there it was: *The Celestine Prophesy*. I had not seen it all these years. I took it out, excited to read it. Here was my first lesson. The second came in the morning.

The following morning, I opened the Course to my next lesson, ACIM, lesson 159: *"I give the miracles I have received."* I read: *"Christ's vision is a miracle"*, it is *"the bridge between the worlds"*, the world of love, heaven-like, and the world of the ego where judgment, hatred, and sin (unworthiness, etc.) abide.

> *What was to be the home of sin (through Christ's vision)... becomes the hearth of mercy, where the suffering are healed and welcome. No one will be turned away from this new home, where his salvation waits. No one is stranger to him. No one asks for anything of him except the gift of his acceptance of his welcoming.* (ACIM Workbook lesson 159, Lines 7.3-6)

I felt the presence of my sobbing, scared little waif, who needed the comforting arms of love and care; these words wrapped around her like a soft cloak. I had done nothing wrong and I was not forever "branded". My ego wanted me to replay this tape of hopelessness, but the Course reminded me:

> *Christ's vision is the holy ground in which the lilies of forgiveness set their roots. This is their home. They can be brought from here back to the world, but they can never grow in its unnourishing and shallow soil. They need the light and warmth and kindly care Christ's charity provides. They need the love with which he looks on them... Take from his storehouse, that its treasures may increase...*
(ACIM, Workbook lesson 159, lines 8.1-9.1)

The more I read the more my little waif ceased crying. Someone was there, someone did love her, and she needed to dry her tears to look around and see that "all was well." And I needed to be aware that beautiful, delicate "*lilies of forgiveness*" for myself and for others cannot survive in the *"unnourishing and shallow soil"* of the world (line 8.3); they need to take their strength from a symbolic other world, a world of Truth, to which Christ's vision becomes "*the bridge*". I needed to tap into something I could not see, but could experience if I desired. That would require faith.

I did not want to "look a gift horse in the mouth." I had been taken care of during my accident the way I had my entire life, even as a child. The more I could open to this possibility, the more I could share the miracle of certainty of care and love with others; as the Course instructs, it is only in teaching that we learn (see ACIM, Manual for Teachers, Introduction). *A Course in Miracles* tells us that in all occurrences and happenings, the central theme is always, *"God's Son is guiltless, and in his innocence is his salvation."*(ACIM, Teacher's Manual, Part I, line 3.5)

My saga of pain, abuse, and abandonment is my ego's story of death, and as I see it played out over and over again, I can see in truth: *"The lady* (or the ego) *doth protest too much".* There is something "over the top" (to quote my ex-husband) in this repetitive "punishment" or bad luck. Perhaps unconsciously I expect bad luck or "punishment." Jean Houston tells of an exchange with the famous anthropologist, Margaret Meade. When asked why she was so lucky in life, the latter responded: *"because I expect to be."*(1)

(1) www.jeanhouston.org

CHAPTER 14

The Decision

Sometimes it's time to make a change…it just is. Perhaps you have known it for a while, but for some reason it wasn't time. You weren't ready; the cake wasn't done. "*You can't hurry growth*", my sister repeatedly said, and in French they say, "*you can't go faster than the music*" ("*on ne peut pas aller plus vite que la musique.*")

Still, when it's time, it's time…or you burn the cake, you're off-beat…no longer in time with the music. That's what my accident showed me. It was time, time to go, time to leave France and to go "home", back to America. I had lived in my adopted country half my life, actually a little over half my life, but lately I had been hemming and hawing and thinking about a way to return to the States. Though my little waif wanted to hole up and hide, it was time.

When it's time, you go; you don't worry about cars, or question whether it's a good time to sell a house…it's time, so you organize to go. That's what I decided to do. I had air miles with Air France, so I got on the phone and ordered a one way ticket to Washington D.C. I had three weeks to get organized.

* * *

What moved me to make this decision after all this time?

In my story there is no "Prince Charming" or "knight in shining armor" who rode in to save the day. As I reflected on my life, particularly the last two years, I realized I had a strong tendency to look back and to think: "*I should have*" done something else. I felt weary from this past, mostly from my judgment on it, not so much from what had actually happened. I realized I had done quite well despite my challenges, and I had never given up. As for making it alone in rural France, I had tried hard for more than two years. My big challenges had begun ten years ago when my husband walked out on Christmas Eve. I could honestly say I had not given up.

It was time for change, a big change; there were no "*ifs, ands, and buts*"… I needed to stop continually judging myself. What had happened, <u>happened</u>. Let it go. Present circumstances did not mean I was "bad", "unworthy", or "incompetent." Those were heavy, incapacitating beliefs I had grown up with as a child, no matter what I did, it was always wrong. Today I could see the indoctrination, and it was time to give it back to those who chose to believe in it, and to stop looking back. I wanted to choose a new thought system and the one proposed in *A Course in Miracles* spoke to me. In this way, I could create a new life, bearing in mind the aim was not to create a better "dream", but "to awaken from the dream". Many months ago I had felt a part of my mission in life was to "see through the illusion"; this expressed a personal goal, and it was time to focus and to practice. Life would happen, and I could not "stop the world, I want to get off," each time things went differently from what I wanted. I needed to be less attached to the outcome. As the Buddhists teach, suffering comes from attachment (grasping and aversion), not the events of life. The car is busted? It is busted. I'll probably have another car at some point in my life.

What were the lessons I wanted to learn from this experience?

*__Be grateful__ you are unscathed and unhurt, as is Brownie. __Be__ grateful, not as a bargain with the universe or God, as a way to prove *"what a good girl I am; I'm doing the lessons I'm supposed to."* Just be grateful, and because this is a new habit, realize it will take <u>practice</u>.

"Fais le ménage" as they say in French. Take stock and **clean out the old**. Pay attention to what you're thinking; it is the script for materialized events. Edgar Cayce said: *"Mind is the builder."* The findings of quantum physics show the same in terms of intention.

*__Be kind__ – particularly to yourself; it'll allow you to be so with others. As lesson 102 in ACIM states in the opening line:

> You do not want to suffer. You may think it buys you something, and may still believe a little that it buys you what you want. Yet this belief is surely shaken now, at least enough to let you question it, and to suspect it really makes no sense.
> (ACIM lesson 102 Para.1)

*__Be gentle__, with your feelings, thoughts, and body…and with our battered world and all its inhabitants. They (peoples, animals, trees and all living creatures) have a right to live in peace, free from abuse. There is no other way than to believe in love, goodness, and kindness (1), and to live accordingly. It's your life; you can change the way you experience it, but you cannot change the events that come your way.

*__Live in the Now__. "This too shall pass."

***Move on.** As a friend and I said in returning from a fun movie, *"something always happens".* Let go of the old so something new can step in, instead of inviting in the old fears and hurts from old beliefs that don't serve.

***Enjoy and live in joy.** Take from life, but only what you need. Remember to share. And as both the Course and Assagioli propose: be joyful! Lesson 93 reminds us: *Light and peace and joy abide in me.*

Be happy, for your only function here is happiness.
(ACIM lesson 102 Para.5, line1)

***Choose peace.** Not easy when the ego wants to be right, but as the Course asks, *"do you prefer to be right or happy?"*

And most of all: **LOVE**. Learn to love, pray for guidance, and know that appearances are deceiving. As Eileen Caddy, a principal co-founder of The Findhorn Foundation in Scotland said:

> *Become channels for love. Love those you are with, love what you are doing, love your environment, and love those who are your seeming enemies. Love the unlovable as well as the lovable. Feel the need for love in every soul and allow yourselves to become channels for love to flow through to meet that need. Let my divine love, that universal love, flow in and through you. When Love is guiding your lives, they will be abundant and fulfilled.*

And finally…**forgive.**

> *Forgive the past and let it go, for it is gone. You stand no longer on the ground that lies between the two worlds. You have gone on, and reached the world that lies at Heaven's gate. There is no hindrance to the Will of God, nor any need that you repeat again a journey that was over long ago. Look gently on your brother, and behold the world in which perception of your hate has been transformed into a world of love.* (2)

---

(1) See Piero Ferrucci, *The Power of Kindness*
(2) ACIM Text, chapter 26 "The Transition", sect. V (lines 14.1-5)

CHAPTER 15

Responsibility
(Parental Guidance suggested)

Ten days after the accident that changed not only my end of year vacation plans, but precipitated my decision to return to America, other things began to settle within me and a deeper understanding to take root.

I spent two weeks "grounded", without a car and without support from the insurance company, the garage where the car had been towed, and the tour operator who had rented me the apartment in Biarritz. Even my so-called friends seemed distant and uninterested; only mere acquaintances were the slightest bit helpful. I viewed these phenomena as further reason to move on. After several days to rest and lick my wounds, I rolled up my sleeves and took matters in hand to examine the extent of car damage, and get on with what had to be done. I also sat down and wrote – my aim was to finish my book.

One morning eating breakfast and listening to a workshop given by Ken and Gloria Wapnick of the *Foundation for a Course in Miracles* (1), I heard information and readings I had already encountered, but never heard in the same way. For some reason, today, I was ready to <u>hear</u> the explanation of human behavior offered through the teachings of the Course. (Perhaps I was ready to hear because at this point there was no alternative). I had been alone – <u>really alone</u> – and cut off without a vehicle for two weeks. This period followed several months of solitude in my little house in the woods. As I listened to the description of the ego thought system, founded on a belief in scarcity, need, "cannibalism" and guilt, I could see the parallel with the relationship I had had with A... At the time I had been convinced I was "in love" with him and he with me. But the last two years' exploration of my psyche had shown me a less glorious, altruistic or "loving" picture.

My "femme fatale" had clearly revealed she was not interested in the house in the suburbs (to quote Caroline Myss), and to have her needs met she could be out for blood! What she wanted far surpassed any desire to give to someone else. Her form of love was seduction in order to meet her own needs. She felt (and through her I experienced) a deep feeling of lack. Since this part of me believed I was lacking, someone else was necessary to complete me. In my life script this was a man, and one that adored and subtly worshipped me.

This was the more obvious ego belief and motivation I lived out in my life. However, on deeper observation (true to the Course's teachings), the game was more bloodthirsty than it appeared. When A. unexpectedly left, I initially felt **I** was to blame, but as I explored my feelings over the months that followed, I saw how livid, angry and enraged I felt within. A part of me felt it was **A.'s** responsibility to do what **I** wanted, to respond to my needs and to give me what I wanted! Look how I had suffered as a child! He was to redeem that wrong, but he had abandoned me. HE was to blame – he was in the wrong, and because of his betrayal and treachery **I** had the right to blame him, and…to demand retribution… *"Behold me brother, at thy hand I die!"* (ACIM T-27.I 4:6)

I had glimpsed this dynamic and hidden need in my relationship with A. when I reflected after our break-up; it had scared me. I was afraid of the depth of my own self-righteous anger. To protect others and myself from such unchristian, though up to now unconscious desires, I had since maintained a distance from people, and particularly men. I did not want to re-experience a "love addicted" relationship now that I could see the gory transaction in action. But, avoiding people, or men in my case, did not remove or deactivate the cause…i.e. the belief in a lack of wholeness and a need to 'cannibalize' others in order to feel complete.

As I listened to *A Course in Miracles* workshop and for the umpteenth time, the explanation of the entire ego thought system of attack, defence and cover-up to maintain innocence, a realization dawned on me… like mist seeping into the dark recesses of my mind. I could see what I had somehow known… the relationship with A. was merely the icing on the cake. The mechanism and ego dynamic was more deeply rooted than what was commonly called a "love addiction." Avoiding or renouncing men was not going to free my mind of the need for:

> *attack, defense; defense, attack (which) become the circles of the hours and the days that bind the mind in heavy bands of steel with iron overlaid, returning but to start again. There*

> *seems to be no break nor ending in the ever-tightening grip of the imprisonment upon the mind. (2)*

This sense of imprisonment I had experienced in my therapy sessions and psychosynthesis work, an image and sensation of the grip of steel bands impossible to undo, so tight is their grip on the beliefs of who I thought I was.

> *Defenses are the costliest of all the prices which the ego would exact. In them lies madness in a form so grim that hope of sanity seems but to be an idle dream, beyond the possible… You are its slave. You know not what you do, in fear of it…who feel its iron grip upon your heart. (3)*

How often had I described the pain in my heart and chest as exactly that: an iron grip that prevented me from breathing freely or taking in breath, the life force ("*prana*" in Sanskrit and yoga).

The workshop continued, and Ken and Gloria's words continued to filter in:

> *The building of a concept of the self is what the learning of the world is for. This is its purpose…A concept of the self is made by you. It bears no likeness to yourself at all…The concept of the self the world would teach is not the thing that it appears to be. For it is made to serve two purposes, but one of which the mind can recognize. The first presents the face of innocence, the aspect acted on. It is this face that smiles and charms and even seems to love. It searches for companions and it looks, at times with pity, on the suffering, and sometimes offers solace. It believes that it is good within an evil world. (4)*

I remembered feeling a victim in my recent car accident. I often felt like a victim, had experienced this feeling my whole life, but felt I was "justified" since I was victimized as a child. Today, my painful past had been recognized and validated in my therapy and psychosynthesis work, but my inability to let the past go, forgive and release old patterns of victimization had also become clear to me. To perpetuate my story, I seemed to have taken on the role of executioner, and to revel in replaying the role of poor abandoned, unloved, forgotten, "thrown in the ditch" little "waif." I used every situation that did not work out for me as a way to 'prove' how victimized I was by outside circumstances, and how unfair life was, to me.

> *Beneath the face of innocence there is a lesson that the concept of the self was made to teach. It is a lesson in a terrible displacement, and a fear so devastating that the face that smiles above it must look away forever, lest it perceive the treachery it hides. The lesson teaches this: "I am the thing you made of me, and as you look on me, you stand condemned because of what I am." (5)*

I could feel a finger clearly pointing at A, and behind in the shadowy sidelines…at both my father and mother. I was the victim, and they were the victimizers. As this section in the Course continues to explain:

> *Here is the central lesson that ensures your brother is condemned eternally. For what you are has now become his sin. For this is no forgiveness possible. No longer does it matter what he does, for your accusing finger points to him, unwavering and deadly in its aim. (6)*

This is how my story served me…to demonstrate "by hook or by crook," that i – the concept of the self created by ego – was right! This part of me was angry… livid… and wanted somebody to pay… pay for ruining my life, destroying my gaiety and replacing it with terror! I was right and I would rerun the story to death to prove it! I was reminded of a starved, neglected little black poodle Bernard and I had 'saved' during one of our walking tours. That little dog had been so traumatized by lack of food and starvation that he never got over it. Even when it was clear we would always feed him, love him and provide a home for him, he could not stop himself from stealing food or picking up revolting maggot-infested, rotting bones in the street. He became ferocious and would bite when we tried to take them away from him; he would not give up the fight. He was so convinced he was right, and it had to be his way.

One evening, sadly, he did his own thing one time too many by running away at night. Bernard found him early the next morning, dead, on a 'quiet' street in our village. Apparently a neighbor heard him whining after a car hit him at midnight, but she was too scared to go out. He died alone in the cold, sometime between the accident at midnight and 7 a.m. when Bernard found him the next day.

We so believe deep within ourselves that we are bad, lacking, and guilty. The small concept of the self created by the ego drums the story into us, and obedient, we never question its validity. We play the story out over and over, almost to convince ourselves of its truth. But we cannot bear to see we are our own victimizers, so we project our upset and unhappiness on the outside environment…our families, employers, governments…anyone will do. In these scenarios, life is never wonderful…there is never enough…and <u>something</u> is always lacking, or not right.

Hidden in my own unconscious, projected onto the people in my life through my script, was my own feeling of guilt. Symbolically, I could see the entire ego dynamic of unworthiness the Course explains. The incomplete and petty concept of the self keeps us from ever encountering the true "Self," resplendent with holiness, light, love, and in essence, divinity. The aim of the small self is to make us suffer since it tells us we are guilty – this is the teaching of our world. We are all guilty and unworthy in some way. To 'protect' us from this unbearable guilt, the ego develops a ploy to deter attention from the real problem or cause of unhappiness: <u>projection of the fault for our circumstances on the outside world.</u>

* * *

Nothing and no one outside ourselves can complete us. We will always be disappointed in someone or something we thought was the answer. No matter what another person does, no matter what we receive in the world, it is never enough. And blindly we continue to use, take and look for more… This explains why love can so easily change to hatred, extreme hatred. I could unexpectedly understand the words: *"And in your suffering of any kind you see your own concealed desire to kill."(7)* If we buy into this belief system, we need to kill or be killed, a projection to protect us from ever looking at the made up horror of our unconscious desires.

Yet, what if it were all made up? The concept we have accepted of "self" in the world is designed to protect us from the fear of unworthiness and a strong belief in guilt. Yet what if the notion itself of guilt and unworthiness were mere hogwash? What if there existed another concept of Self? *"Ideas leave not their source,"*(8) is a central theme in the Course. What is our source? All the spiritual teachings I had ever read, teach we are part of a larger whole. A drop of water, though single and individual, is still water, carrying all the elements of 'water'. *A Course in Miracles* teaches us we have not left our Source... Being an effect of God, we can choose a more peaceful, happier way of experiencing life. In place of the ego's construct of guilt, suffering, attack and retribution, we can accept a kinder, more loving story since *"you have no need to be less loving to God's Son than He Whose Love created him as loving as Himself."* (ACIM lesson 102 para5. line 2)

According to the Course, I was an "idea in the mind of God." Lesson 110 teaches: *"I am as God created me."*

> *Today's idea is therefore all you need to let complete correction heal your mind, and give you perfect vision that will heal all the mistakes that any mind has made at any time or place. It is enough to heal the past and make the future free. It is enough to let the present be accepted as it is. It is enough to let time be the means for all the world to learn escape from time, and every change that time appears to bring in passing by...*
>
> *"I am as God created me. His Son can suffer nothing. And I am His Son."*
>
> *Then, with this statement firmly in your mind, try to discover in your mind the Self Who is the holy Son of God Himself.* (ACIM Workbook lesson 110 Para 2.1-4; Para 6-7)

What a possibility? I could accept this belief...or hang onto the previously unconscious thought system that had run my life thus far. And what if my whole life's *"mise en scène"* was designed to bring me to this discovery?

* * *

When placing your finger on a damning and frightening possibility concerning unconscious motivations and drives, an initial reaction may be such intense fear that denial, flight, or a well-known distraction may be preferred in the place of looking and allowing. Ice cream, alcohol, drugs, and work...anything must be better. But, at some point it's time to face ourselves and the beliefs that drive our lives. We're all in this together; we have followed the same ego injunction, regardless of the form it takes in our lives. We are not bad, just misled. *A Course in Miracles* instructs in an awakening to a "happy dream", to no longer allow retribution or guilt to plunge you into the well-known dens of avoidance, forgetting, and projection. Using 'will' and the psychosynthesis practice of dis-identification, I decided it was time to choose comfort in remembering:

> *Everyone here has entered darkness, yet no one has entered it alone. Nor need he stay more than an instant. For he has come with Heaven's Help within him, ready to lead him out of darkness into light at any time. The time he chooses can be any time, for help is there, awaiting but his choice. (9)*

---

(1) *Foundation for A Course in Miracles*, Temecula, Ca. www.facim.org
   Numerous books and taped workshops are available to clarify the teachings of the Course.
(2) ACIM, workbook lesson 153 lines 3.2-3
(3) ACIM workbook lesson 153 lines 4.1-5.4
(4) ACIM text, chapter 31.V.5-2.9
(5) ACIM, text, chapter 31.V. 5.1-3
(6) ACIM, text chapter 31.V. 6.1-4
(7) ACIM text chapter 31.V.15. Line 10
(8) ACIM, text, chapter 26.VII. 4.7
(9) ACIM text, chapter 25.III. 6.1-4

CHAPTER 16

"My present happiness is all I see."

(ACIM Workbook Lesson 290)

The past is over. It is, yet we hang on to it in our minds so desperately that it seems it is not over. In truth we merely reprogram and replay an ingrained past belief or response to life. It was months later…I had returned to my little house in the woods in the south of France. I found the Washington area "unnatural, fake, noisy, crowded, and too rushed" for my liking. Fortunately my little house had not sold, so I returned early April, just in time to enjoy a glorious spring and easy summer. I felt stronger, content to be alone, and happy to be in nature. Mostly I relied upon myself, spent time alone, and relished the sweet smelling air, the return of warm, long days, and the virtuoso birdsong that enlivened my mornings and evenings. I settled in, planted flowers, cleaned my back terrace, got out warm weather gear, and started life again in a small, simple village in southwest France. My yoga classes picked up as if nothing had disturbed their schedule, only more people came.

Summer arrived and I began to swim in the outdoor lakes. The tango festival returned in July and though I had not danced for a year, a serendipitous event brought me a gentle, talented partner on a silver platter. I danced and glowed for two weeks, feeling more and more relaxed, in tune with myself and trusting of others; my "dancer" was on cloud nine! Things were working; life was sweet. Still, I felt unsettled. I could not let go of America, missing my own kind, needing community, and wanting to speak English. But, I focused on a life in France and explored the possibility of building a small extension onto my little house. I went out from time to time with people, and even ventured meeting men.

The days were beautiful, the nights soft, my time my own. I had a few coaching clients and felt nourished by the service I offered – I loved working with these women! Somehow during each session I could hear and understand their predicament, and in each session a relaxing/loosening took place and they were more at peace, less tight, and ready to move on with life.

These sessions grounded and centered me as well. Though our stories and life roles were different, I could relate to what my clients said. One client in Paris seemed almost like a twin; she had travelled similar waters to my own, though the storyline was different. The fear of not being good enough despite earth-shattering efforts, the need for a man to help and define one, and the feeling of being stuck in the cloggy muck of self doubt and guilt was all too familiar…wanting to step out and be independent, but somehow <u>not being able to</u> no matter how much intellectual understanding existed about the paralysing effects of past parental and childhood shaming.

So the past was **not** over. Loyalty to our parents' teaching and indoctrination is laudatory, **and** paralysing. It seems to take much time to remove the sticky strings of filial obedience. We think we are free, living our own lives, but within, we play out once again a belief in inadequacy, a script of financial insecurity, broken relationships and/or fear of emotional intimacy. Despite the positive changes in my way of approaching and receiving life, I could see I was still hanging on (for dear life) to the need for a safe, non-threatening environment of peace, quiet, isolation, and…boredom. I was not happy, and enforced solitude was not exactly the way I wanted to live. There were many aspects I adored, particularly living in pristine nature; that is what kept me where I was. I ruminated about how much I could lose by letting go of my little house in the woods.

One sunny morning, while wandering down to the farmer's market in town, I felt that selling my house was like a death. If I did it, I could not turn back, like in the Greek myth leaving Hades, the advice is <u>not</u> to turn and look back despite what you hear, or don't hear… How many times had I made plans, made a decision, then begun to "look back" (in my mind) and felt paralysed? Selling my little house was like a death… I had been trying to avoid that. Perhaps I was even bargaining with life by saying: *"if I build an extension, then it'll be **my** house, not the house I built with ex-husband 16 years ago… and this little village will be <u>mine</u>, not the village we came to explore, wide-eyed and in puppy love, 19 years ago."*

Death…letting go, moving on – I did not feel experienced at this. I had always hung on to the little I had, clinging to a belief I had been taught: *"you don't deserve, or don't count much, so be happy with what you get, and don't waste it."* This had been clear in the food and clothing I received, and in the lack of extras or presents – gifts were always utilitarian and money was only spent on what you needed. Here I was, 51 years of age, still playing out the same 'teaching', unable to let go of what I had, for fear of being deemed <u>ungrateful</u>, subsequently receiving nothing and having to go without.

Not having enough to take care of myself…clothes, food and most importantly a home where I was safe…was a terrifying fear that haunted me. That was the root of my fear: *"I was ungrateful"*… bad and awful that I dared ask for something I did not have (!), dared to be unhappy with what I did have… The teaching was ingrained and alive. I had covered it up so no one would find it, because if they <u>did</u> find it, it would show I had <u>dared</u> be dissatisfied with my lot, thus proving I <u>was</u> ungrateful and bad – **that** was a crime worthy of death!

As I uncovered these beliefs, I could not hear parental voices from the past, or even remember any particular incidents. This way of being permeated my entire childhood, like an entrenched odor you simply become accustomed to. That was the way it had been; both my grandmother and parents had taught me to be grateful for what you have, and to certainly not <u>want</u>, let alone <u>ask</u>, for anything else. I had integrated the lesson well. I was good at getting by with little, accepting the professional circumstances and people that came into my life; this way I could have something…better than nothing. But it was no wonder I had a hard time letting things go…ex-husband, old clothes and furniture, A. (a man who did not suit me), and a little house in an environment that no longer served my needs.

The teaching was at work, and what upheld and maintained it was insidious and hidden: <u>guilt</u>…that old "friend," guilt. My Paris client brushed up against its back during our last coaching session and recoiled in fear as guilt flashed her a recriminating glance. Our belief of "not being good enough" to do something or be someone, is deep-seated. We're somehow guilty and terrified that this is true. Guilt keeps us in line with family injunctions or family teachings, and guilt keeps the past alive. We all struggle with it, that feeling of being guilty, not deserving. As Ken Wapnick suggests, watch your reaction the next time you're driving and you see flashing lights in your rear view mirror.

The past is over. It can touch me not.

Unless the past is over in my mind, the real world must escape my sight. For I am really looking nowhere; seeing but what is not there. How can I then perceive the world forgiveness offers? This the past was made to hide, for this the world that can be looked on only now. It has no past. For what can be forgiven but the past, and if it is forgiven it is gone.

"Father, let me not look upon a past that is not there. For You have offered me Your Own replacement, in a present world the past has left untouched and free of sin. Here is the end of guilt. And here am I made ready for Your final step. Shall I demand that You wait longer for Your Son to find the loveliness You planned to be the end of all his dreams and all his pain?" (ACIM, workbook lesson 289)

CHAPTER 17

Taking Time...
When it's time...

Summer

I awake before 6 a.m. I get up to go to the bathroom, then return to bed. Brownie is ready to come up for his early morning cuddle, but is patient, always waiting for my invitation to jump up on the bed. I love to cuddle him, and he snuggles his back against my tummy and emits little sounds of contentment.

Joy. Before sleeping, I read again in *The Power of Kindness* about Roberto Assagioli's relationship with joy, a relationship he sought and cultivated, similar to one with a person or other living being. (1) Brownie is a happy boy and spontaneously demonstrates his joy with unexpected spurts of barking, tail wagging, and sudden running in circles. He often does this at the lake – perhaps the mirroring effect of water catalyses the ever-present state of joy and sends it bubbling and bursting forth! Brownie certainly merits his nickname, "Bubbly," pure bubbling joy. I feel a steady bubbling myself this morning. I cannot stay in bed though I am conscious of my little "waif," whose tendency is to hide under the safe, warm covers. I see how much she needs cuddling, reassurance, and love, just like Brownie. With this reassurance and love, she too may allow that natural state of joy to pour forth. Joy…in place of fear. I prefer the exchange, and understand I have another practice to develop: <u>cultivating joy</u>.

I am grateful to Dr. Assagioli and psychosynthesis for teaching and showing me other ways of being. I understand today how the journey to reclaim Self, to encounter Self, takes time. When I started working with psychosynthesis more than two years ago, I wanted the pain gone, the exploration over and done with, so I could "get on with life," "move on," "get a life". Now I see this **is** my life. I came back to my little house in southwest France after a few months in the U.S. I felt a call for quiet, fewer people, sweet, fresh air, and nature… <u>green</u>: trees, leaves, grass… <u>blue</u>: sky and water… <u>brown</u>: fallen leaves, industrious, ever busy ants, long-legged, graceful spiders.

Mostly I felt a need for quiet and stillness, the sounds of the wind ranging from a slight breeze to the strong rustling of leaves in the trees. I missed the birdsong…and have I been blessed with birdsong! I feel like I live in a bird sanctuary, where I am serenaded by inimitable, original, joyous operetta morning and evening. Yesterday, as I wrote outdoors in the playful breeze, I was privy to the courting song and dance of a colourful and demonstrative male wood tit appealing to his less receptive and quieter *Dulcinea*. What a gift!

I needed time, time to allow myself to emerge, to unfold, and to **be**. This time has been a gift. I am grateful that despite relentless 'imperatives' that push me to perform, function, compete, move, "get on with life," I stopped and took my own time. The Course says time's sole purpose is *"the awakening of God's Son"*…*"time waits upon forgiveness that the things of time may disappear because they have no use."*(2) Both the Course and author, Louise Hay teach:

> *It's time to forgive ourselves, and set ourselves free… Forgiveness means giving up our hurtful feelings and letting the whole thing go.*
>
> *When we won't forgive, when we won't let go, we're binding ourselves to the past, and when we are stuck in the past we cannot live in present time, and if we are not living in the present, how can we create our glorious future? Old garbage from the past just creates more garbage from the future. (3)*

In her work, Hay identifies four major blocks that hold us tied to our stories and our past: <u>criticism, fear, guilt and resentment</u>. Whatever our blocks to life and to happiness, they always reveal an inability to forgive.

> *An unforgiving thought is one which makes a judgment that it will not raise to doubt, although it is not true. The mind is closed, and will not be released. The thought protects projection, tightening its chains, so that distortions are more veiled and more obscure; less easily accessible to doubt, and further kept from reason. (4)*

Forgiveness is the only way to peace and to discovering Self. I understand that better today, and realize the understanding will deepen with time. Everything that happens in our lives happens for a reason, if we take the time to reflect, let go of the judgment, understand, and integrate the learning. We are not forgotten or unloved, though a frightened or angry part of ourselves may turn somersaults to persuade us we are. To know and <u>experience</u> this knowing, the way I know water will support me when I swim, we must learn to listen to, care for ourselves, and to trust. We all have a doorway to ourselves. Perhaps we have padlocked and barricaded it, even forgotten where the door lies! Yet, if we slow down and stop running after unsubstantial glittery toys and useless trinkets of possession, we will (in time and with time) encounter a true treasure of joy, understanding, peace, and love.

* * *

My little "waif" is timid, often frightened, sometimes frozen and unable to move. I need not judge and abuse her with reproachful looks or words. The "off with her head" Queen believes in moving on, getting things done, and creating a place for herself in the world. But is that pushy, aggressive side of me equally not veiling fear, instead of a clear and strong sense of Self? Psychosynthesis teaches us to welcome, embrace and grow the different parts of our internal family, so we can stop pushing, fighting and hating ourselves. Pushing, taunting and shouting at a scared little person doesn't ever get us what we want; it didn't work when my father did it when I was a child, and it doesn't work today. As one of my clients said recently: *"it's like working with a scared and wounded cat. You put out food, leave it alone, and wait. When the cat is ready, she comes to eat."* And that is the beginning of the relationship.

When we are ready, we find the door to ourselves. Perhaps we merely look at it in astonishment the first time, and then walk away. In time, we return. With time, taking time, we begin to remove the heavy locks, oil the hinges, and locate the key to open this weighty, long forgotten door to our Selves. Like the story of a princess betrothed to a dragon that Jack Kornfield recounts in his book, *After the Ecstasy, the Laundry*, peeling away layers of false identities, survival personalities and roles can be painful; coming out of hiding and denial is the only way to discover who we truly are. This shedding is the work of a lifetime, our ultimate symphony or masterpiece, journey to a sacred inner marriage, the meeting of 'yin' and 'yang', the reclaiming of Self. It takes time, will begin, and continue in time. We need not judge ourselves for being late, push or prod, torture or abuse; instead we need to let go, open, trust, listen, and ask.

In the words of Tiny Tim in Charles Dickens's *A Christmas Carol:* "God bless us, one and all." And may I wish you, *bon voyage* on your own amazing journey.

THE END

(1) Piero Ferrucci, *The Power of Kindness*, chapter "Joy", pps.253-254
(2) ACIM, text -29. VI.2: 14
(3) Louise Hay, *The Power is Within You*, (pps 60, 90, 113)
(4) ACIM workbook, part II.1 *What is Forgiveness?* Lines 2.1-3

Post Scriptum
When re-reading my manuscript for corrections before going to print a year after writing, I could see that I glossed over an understanding of the need to grieve the loss of my childhood, and the pain experienced by my mortally terrified, little waif, 'Morteresse'. She truly believed she was unlovable, but was so afraid of this possibility that she did everything to run from the realization.

The fear to face this eventuality actually protected her from a thought that anyone so vile and contemptible as to be unlovable by his or her own parents, should be removed from the world. As an adult, with a lot of internal work and healing under my belt, the belief and fear of such vileness and shame, still brought such alarm to me that if true, the thought jumped into my mind I should thrust a dagger through my own heart. Interesting how in my meditations the pain in my chest often appeared to me as a symbolic dagger stabbed through my heart.

I understand now that 'Morteresse' was truly terrified at the thought that she **was** unlovable, and had potentially absorbed that belief from her father, who undoubtedly feared the same. In this way she hoped to protect him from such abhorrent terror, thus showing the depth of her own humanness, compassion, and love, and in so doing demonstrating the contrary of the ghastly fear that consumed and haunted her, her entire life.

May we dwell in the heart.
May we be free from suffering;
May we be healed.
May we be filled with love.
May we be at peace.
May we be happy.
(Buddhist prayer of loving kindness)

Afterword

Thanks to this inward journey and courage to look within, I have something I never believed possible: a sense of "Self"... my own self, with its weaknesses, talents and strengths, and a link to a greater transpersonal, ever-present, Loving Self. I am no longer terrified to be alone, or afraid of non-existence. I feel more philosophical about life and in general, much more peaceful about whatever comes my way. Then, there are other days when I forget, or lose contact...

My journey, unfinished, is just beginning. There were difficult and frightening times, as in any journey. Where will it lead me? Time will tell, but one thing is sure. As Melville said: *"where I am going is on no map; no true place is."* In the past, there were times when I did not believe I would "make it", I felt so decidedly useless, unworthy, and without being. I <u>have</u> made it, meaning today I have met myself and am pleased, but the battle is far from won. There are days when the teachings of psychosynthesis and the practice of disindentification allow me to touch that part of Self which is pure awareness and will; then there are other times when the battle between my conflicting subpersonalities wears me out and brings me to tears.

"Child abuse casts a shadow the length of a lifetime." (1) I understand from experience what this means. Abuse of any kind is de-humanizing, demeaning, belittling – it makes the recipient an object for the use and gain of the perpetrator. This is true whether we speak of children, animals, or adults of any sex, creed, color or culture. Why is it that in the 21st century, with our so-called advanced technologies, we are underdeveloped in our consciousness and abilities to relate to ourselves and other living beings? Marianne Williamson recounts a story in one of her lectures about the day a child comes home from school and tells her parents of an unbelievable tale her teacher told in school. She tells her parents the teacher said that once, a long, long time ago, there was something called "war" in which people killed each other and fought to harm other nations because of differences of opinion, or because they wanted something the other nation had. The little girl in disbelief says, *"tell me, this is not possible – did it really once exist?"*

I hope and pray that one day, children will ask not only if war ever existed, but if it is true that parents or other family members inflicted physical pain on children, used them for their own sexual pleasure, or in other ways disrespected and dishonored their spirit and being. I hope and pray that one day, we will joyfully <u>honor</u> other peoples and their right to different beliefs, values and goals, that we will learn the only way to survive and advance on this earth is through **understanding, acceptance, empathy, and love,** and that we will learn to communicate in a non-violent way (2) and to honor all beings whether they speak our language or not.

I hope and pray that we will learn to respect life in its form of animals, plant, or human being…that we will see the joy and beauty in the expression of the life force, and that we will relinquish our need to dominate, use and abuse in order to give ourselves a sense of worth or purpose. How can we believe we are <u>always</u> right? Humility and concern for all sentient beings would change the face of this world dramatically, and allow us to live in peace and serenity.

Let us, to quote Gandhi: *"Be in the world what you want to see in the world."* And, to **be** in the world, embark on your own journey, explore and discover who you are, uncover and reclaim your true Self…awaken to who you are. Let go of judgment and the belief you are right. Forgive people you believe have wronged you. Forgive yourself for your own unkind, harsh words and actions.

Workbook lesson 335 from *A Course in Miracles* reminds us:
Forgiveness is a choice. I never see my brother as he is, for that is far beyond perception. What I see in him is merely what I wish to see, because it stands for what I want to be the truth… What could restore Your memory to me, except to see my brother's sinlessness? His holiness reminds me that he was created one with me, and like myself. **In him I find my Self…** *(My bold)*

Ultimately what is the aim of this life, and what is most important?
Where would I go but Heaven? What could be a substitute for happiness? What gift could I prefer before the peace of God? What treasure would I seek and find and keep that can compare with my Identity? And would I rather live with fear than love? (ACIM workbook lesson 287)

Guilt and shame is the jailor. A cruel driver, shame and guilt keep us in terror, convinced of an unquestioned and unquestionable belief in sin or personal lack. Our guilt need not be based on anything horrendous, but is experienced as horribly shaming. And this shame holds and controls our entire lives. Look at the example in the film "*The Reader*", where the heroine is willing to be imprisoned for life, unwilling is she to admit her inability to read. In our world until we choose to awaken, it is to guilt, an intractable slave master and god, to whom we cower and bow. Fortunately, we have a choice and another way, but it is up to each of us to make it.

(1) The Tennyson Center for Children, Denver, CO website
(2) Marshall Rosenberg, *Non-Violent Communication*
   (Association for Non-Violent Comunication, Santa Fe, N.M.)

Bibliography & Resources

Psychosynthesis:
Dr Roberto Assagioli,
(1991) *Transpersonal Development, The Dimension beyond Psychosynthesis*, The Aquarian Press
(2002) *The Act of Will, A Guide to Self-Actualisation and Self-Realisation*, Turnstone Press
Molly Young Brown,
(1993) *Growing Whole*, Psychosynthesis Press
(2004) *Unfolding Self, The Practice of Psychosynthesis*, Allworth Press
John Firman and Ann Gila,
(2002) *Psychosynthesis: A Psychology of the Spirit*, SUNY Press
Piero Ferrucci,
(2004) *What We May Be*, Penguin Group
(2007) *The Power of Kindness, The Unexpected Benefits of Leading a Compassionate Life*, Penguin
Diana Whitmore,
(1992) *Psychosynthesis Counselling in Action*, Sage Publications

Psychosynthesis and Education Trust (P.E.T.) in London, UK (Founded by Roberto Assagioli) Provides workshops, trainings and other resources.
Centre Source, *Ecole française de psychosynthèse*, Paris, France
The Findhorn Foundation (Spiritual community in Scotland practicing eco-psychology, psychosynthesis & sustainability)
www.findhorn.org

Works inspired by the teachings of *A Course in Miracles*:
For a complete list of books, taped lectures, and regular workshops see The Foundation for a Course in Miracles, in Temecula, CA
www.facim.org
Marianne Williamson, (2002) *Everyday Grace*, Riverhead Books
(1994) *Illuminata*, Random House
(Prayers and rites to inspire and support)

Books on symbolic sight:
Compilation edited by Molly Young Brown and Carolyn Wilbur Treadway (2009) *Held in Love*, Psychosynthesis Press
Dean Delis and Cassandra Phillips (1990) *The Passion Paradox*, Bantam
Viktor Frankl (1984) *Man's Search for Meaning*, Touchstone Books
Eugene T. Gendlin (2003) *Focusing, How to gain direct access to your body's knowledge*, 25th edition Rider
Louise L. Hay (1991) *The Power is Within You*, Eden Grove Ed.
Caroline Myss (2002) *Sacred Contracts*, Bantam Books
(1996) *Anatomy of the Spirit, The Seven Stages of Power and Healing*, Crown Publishers
Michel Odoul (2003) *Dis-moi où tu as mal (Le lexique)*, ed. Albin Michel
Susan S. Trout (1990) *To See Differently*, Three Roses Press
Mike Burke & Pierre Sarda (2007) *Emergence des valeurs féminines dans l'entreprise, Une révolution en marche*, De Boeck & Larcier

Works on archetypes and subpersonalities:
Caroline Myss (2002) *Sacred Contracts*, Bantam books
Clarissa Pinkola Estès (1992) *Women Who Run with the Wolves: Contacting the power of the wild woman*, Random House
John Firman and Ann Gila, (2002) *Psychosynthesis: A Psychology of the Spirit*, SUNY Press

Non-violent Communication:
Marshall Rosenberg, (2003) *Non-Violent Communication, A Language of Life*, Puddle Dancer Press Book

Discovering Self, Service, and Healing:
Helen Brenner, (2003) *I Know I'm in There Somewhere*, Gotham Books (Fabulous, very useful book)
Rebecca Linder Hintze, (2006) *Healing Your Family History*, Hay House
Jack Kornfield, (2001) *After the Ecstasy, the Laundry (How the Heart Grows Wise on the Spiritual Path)* Bantam

Joanna Macy and Molly Y. Brown, (1998) *Coming back to Life, Practices to Reconnect Our Lives, Our World,* New Society Publishers.
Ram Dass and Mirabai Bush, (1992) *Compassion in Action,* Bell Tower
Wayne Muller, (1992) *Legacy of the Heart, The Spiritual Advantages of a Painful Childhood,* Fireside (extremely insightful)

Resources & Organizations Working to Alleviate Child Abuse
Childhelp, www.childhelp.org
The Tennyson Center for Children, www.tennysoncenter.org
The Norma Morris Center- Adult Survivors of Child Abuse (ASCA) www.ascasupport.org

About the author:
American, the author has lived most of her adult life in France. A transformational coach and guide, she uses psychosynthesis, yoga, dance, and communion with nature to accompany individuals seeking to go beyond societal and family conditioning in order to discover and express their potential, encounter Self, and realize their deepest dreams and desires.

For more information on transformational coaching, training and accompaniment in reclaiming Self, please visit ***www.inner-discovery.com*

www.ingramcontent.com/pod-product-compliance
Lightning Source LLC
Chambersburg PA
CBHW031253290426
44109CB00012B/563